77 Best
Practices in
Negotiation

77
Best Practices in Negotiation

Dr. Gary S. Goodman

Published 2020 by Gildan Media LLC
aka G&D Media
www.GandDmedia.com

Front cover design by David Rheinhardt of Pyrographx

Interior design by Meghan Day Healey of Story Horse, LLC

Library of Congress Cataloging-in-Publication Data is available upon request

ISBN: 978-1-7225-0196-9

10   9   8   7   6   5   4   3   2   1

Contents

Epilogue

When I've Blown It—
A Negotiator's Retrospective 175

Introduction

In negotiations, there is a script that is supposed to be followed.

It isn't written out in so many words, but it's there in the minds of participants. It's an idealized rendering of various scenarios.

Then there is what really happens.

And just as the best-laid plans for a battle never quite prepare you for a conflict, forcing you to adapt under stressful and distracting circumstances, you need to be flexible when approaching your bargaining encounters.

You need *lots* of tools, techniques, strategies, ploys, feints, and bluffs in order to come out on top. That's why I'm providing you with no fewer than 77 Best Practices.

I've paid a fairly steep price to develop these hard-earned ways of getting more of what you want and need. I hope they work as well for you as they have for me, and for the many people I've taught in my "Best Practices in

Negotiation" seminars in and out of extension programs at such distinguished schools at the University of California at Berkeley, UC Davis, and UCLA.

Seldom in a negotiation will you come out giving and getting exactly what you want. And almost always, the negotiation itself will leave some scar tissue.

Like when I was surfing in Hawaii. I was an incompetent competing for waves with the locals, who were increasingly inhospitable as I seemed to ruin wave after wave for them.

Their heckling was sufficient to strip me of my skills, and it didn't help my concentration when some coral speared my shoulder. Gorgeous ocean, full of joyous possibilities, yet none were realized. I'm happy I didn't crawl out of paradise with even more damage to my sports ego and my body.

Some of your negotiations will go this way. They'll be blowouts. You'll hate the folks you're bargaining with. They'll hate you. You'll all lose.

Most books about negotiating tap-dance around human nature, especially the bleak side of it, when people do utterly stupid, self-defeating, and mutually defeating things to ruin what could have been very decent deals.

Not this book.

I'll celebrate some of my wins in the pages to come, but I'll also be the first to tell you when, where, and how I blew it. To really grasp the best practices, you need to learn about some of the worst, taking the sweet with the sour. Otherwise you won't be prepared for the cut and thrust—the full enchilada, the real deal.

Some of my 77 Best Practices have been published as articles. Most of them are about 500 words or less. I'm a big believer in economy of expression, making my point fast and concisely. This means you'll be able to race through a number of pointers in any given reading session.

I hope you'll find this type of reading liberating and very satisfying. You can pass over ideas that seem familiar to you, seeking those that have something entirely new and counterintuitive to teach.

You can pick up and put down this book at will, reading it in almost any order you choose, without losing coherence, because each Best Practice stands on its own.

Let me know how this book helps you, and feel free to contact me with your questions and negotiation challenges.

I coach and consult for individuals and organizations, so if there is a lot on the line, give me a holler.

Gary S. Goodman, PhD, JD, MBA
President
The Goodman Organization, Inc.
www.customersatisfaction.com
gary@customersatisfaction.com
drgaryscottgoodman@yahoo.com
gary@drgarygoodman.com
gary@negotiationschool.com
(818) 970-GARY (4279)

Chapter 1

What Is a Negotiation?

What is a negotiation? When does it begin and end? How does it differ from other transactions, such as everyday buying and selling? And why does it deserve special study, preparation, practice, and investment?

I define negotiation as a *value-for-value exchange, where the values tendered by the parties are variable, subject to the estimation, calculation, and agreement of the parties.*

You walk into a department store and find a nice sweater. The price is $89, according to the tag. You bring it to the register, pay for it in cash, and leave with the item.

This is a transaction, but it isn't a negotiation, according to the definition I have supplied. The store set a price, you paid that price, and the clerk accepted it. The value you gave for the garment, $89, was not bargained for. It wasn't a variable. It was a fixed, predetermined amount.

Had you noticed an imperfection in the weave, you might have pointed this out to the clerk or to the manager, and that flaw might have provided a justification for a price reduction, had you requested one.

At that moment, when you determined you wanted to pay less for the sweater and undertook to seek a reduction, formulating your communication strategy, *negotiation* got underway.

Clerks and managers are commonly empowered to take off a certain percentage from damaged goods, often 10–15 percent. Had they done so, we most certainly would regard the encounter as a negotiation.

But what if they declined to drop the price? Would it still be a negotiation? Yes, because they would have taken a position—that the sweater was still worth full price— or they might have puffed, "We're not that kind of store!"

You would then have the option of capitulating or refusing to buy. From your view, if you didn't achieve the desired price, it might not have been a successful negotiation, but it was one nevertheless.

You can see from this example that buying and selling do not always, or often, involve negotiating. But when one party wants to sweeten a deal, gain an additional benefit, avoid a detriment, add certain requirements or conditions, or achieve a discount or obtain payment that is above list price, then negotiation kicks in, like a generator when the lights go out.

When *exactly* does negotiation begin? For those that always pay full price, or accept the values others impose on goods and services as irrevocably fixed, the answer could virtually be, "Never!"

To such folks, nothing seems negotiable. They seek employment, send out résumés, and when they are interviewed and hear the words, "We pay X dollars per year," they reflexively and agreeably say, "Great!"

They don't actively try to improve their lot, because many feel undeserving of special treatment and consideration, or they might be concerned that asking for more will appear greedy and they'll risk losing the job offer.

Others that believe that everything is negotiable and act accordingly. Some proudly declare: "I *never* pay retail prices!" feeling that when they do, they're behaving foolishly, like suckers.

The rest of us fall somewhere in the middle, appreciating that a car dealership is a venue where haggling is expected, and if you don't do at least some of it, you'll get fleeced. But we may blanch at the suggestion of trying to get a casket for a relative's funeral at a reduced price, because that would be simply "unseemly."

These three types of negotiators—the "never bargain," "always bargain," and "sometimes bargain" individuals—are already negotiating their expectations. They are setting certain aspiration levels without necessarily being aware of what they're doing.

Likewise, those that think they can get great deals if they actively seek them out often find they are right, as are the folks that think they can get very little in the way of bargains.

As I explain in Best Practice 36, "The more you ask for, the more you'll get." Not only does behavioral research support this finding, but this phenomenon confirmed in actual practice.

Some wrongly believe, "The more modest I am in my requirements, the more likely it is they'll be fulfilled." That's simply naive. I suspect that this contention stems more from low self-esteem than from negotiation doctrine, but it does dramatize the fact that *negotiations begin in our minds.*

Thus it pays to think through our tacit beliefs about bargaining, its opportunities, obstacles, attractions, and repulsions. We need to adjust the beliefs that are short-changing us.

And when does a negotiation END?

By this point, you're probably about to guess, "Later than I thought!" and you'd be right.

I'm tempted to quote the inimitable Yogi Berra, who said "It ain't over till it's over," appending what an anonymous pundit added: "And it's never over!"

Number 15 of the 77 Best Practices offers this gem from Dun & Bradstreet: "The deal isn't made until the money is paid."

If you take this to heart, as I do, then you'll never leave a transaction with a handshake or even a signed contract, and conclude, "This negotiation is over!"

As you'll see when I outline the anatomy of a negotiation transaction, the sixth step requires *action and execution.* Agreements need to be put into effect, and their conditions need to be met before we can say that a negotiation is concluded.

Let me offer a recurring illustration of this precept. I'm a big sports fan, and I follow professional baseball, basketball, and to a lesser extent, football. (In the case of football, I am much more attentive to college teams.)

One thing I have noticed is when a pro athlete has an unexpectedly productive year, it's common for his or her agent to approach the team's management and invite them to a "renegotiation session." Usually the agent will be seeking a contract extension at a higher rate of pay, but its effective date will be accelerated to the present.

In contract law terms, the agent's client has a preexisting duty to honor the current contract and to play for the amount of money he agreed to beforehand. There is no obligation on the part of team management to accede to the agent's request for an immediate upgrade in pay.

But in the real world of pro sports, everyone knows that an unhappy player simply won't play his best, whether it results from an intention to "do the slow walk," to "dog it," to not hustle and put out 100 percent, or it is simply an unconscious reaction to feeling unappreciated or mistreated.

Thus the athlete's original negotiation still isn't over, even in the middle of its agreed-to contract years, although he is playing and the team is paying. If his agent says, "Stick 'em up!" that original negotiation is subject to being reopened and modified.

Retaining the other party's goodwill, trust, and desire to cooperate is an essential component of effective negotiating. Unfortunately, when a more narrow view of when negotiations begin and end is used, these dynamics are not given the attention, study, or importance they deserve.

Why should we study negotiation at all?

Negotiation is a frequent and significant activity of businesspeople and consumers. Like breathing, it is ignored and mostly taken for granted until the air is noticeably fouled or our lungs spasm.

When negotiations break down, suddenly we're interested in asking, "What went wrong?" But until and unless dysfunction occurs, we rarely bother to study it.

Fortunately, you can find the topic presented in some university extension and continuing-education programs, and through a few commercial providers. I run my course, "Best Practices in Negotiation," at UCLA and UC Berkeley Extension, and privately by invitation at organizations and trade and professional associations worldwide.

I hope this book will make you a more conscious, capable, and comfortable negotiator. But your education doesn't have to stop here, with this text. I invite you to contact me about coaching and consulting as well as opportunities to bring my training to your site.

Chapter 2

Anatomy of a Negotiation

You sidle your car to a gas pump, insert your charge card, fill, and you feel or hear a click, indicating that your tank is topped off. Returning the pump hose to its holder, you get in the car and drive away.

This is more or less how a gasoline purchase *transaction* occurs. If you do these things step-by-step, you'll fill your tank and keep motoring.

Most gas-ups are uneventful. We don't have to outsmart or trick the pumps. We get what we pay for, denominated to the penny. And typically, unless we're fleet customers, we don't dicker over prices or seek discounts.

Most negotiations are also rather smooth and perfunctory transactions. They have beginnings, middles, and ends. We'll discuss these features, identifying six steps that are common to most successful negotiations, steps that you'll want to emulate. But before we do, let me make a few preliminary comments about negotiation and about this book.

Negotiations typically involve two or more parties that are seeking to fulfill some fairly mundane objectives. For example, employers interview prospective employees. The former and the latter need each other, so they're hoping the result of their get-together will be productive.

While the boss (in theory) wants to pay the lowest of all possible salaries, and her new hire wants to earn the highest, generally market forces and the relative urgency each party brings to fulfilling her needs will inform the salary bargaining range.

No matter how clever one party is in negotiation, the worker, practically speaking, cannot accept a post that won't pay her bills, and the manager cannot exceed rationality by offering an exorbitant pay package.

Even if such a lopsided outcome occurred, it wouldn't be sustainable. Sooner or later, and probably sooner, somebody would notice that an error was made.

"What was I thinking?" one person might wake up to realize.

So implicitly an invisible hand will be steering many negotiations, as economists describe the constraints of supply and demand in a free marketplace. There is only so much wiggling room when it comes to setting and getting certain prices and benefits from our bargains.

If bargaining were a baseball game, your team couldn't expect to hurl no-hitters and beat opponents by a score of 15–0 every time they take the field. You'll probably score, and the other team will too. And you'll both make a couple of errors or stupid plays during your time between the lines of the baseball diamond.

Just as there are professional coaches to help you to realize your personal potential, enhance your skills, and provide you with an edge by sharing their wisdom, there are consultants (such as your author) that are here to help you to achieve more than you otherwise would on the basis of your native gifts and range of experiences.

This doesn't mean with my help you'll win every negotiation contest, nor does it mean you'll prevail on every point.

I hope that by reading this book and implementing its wisdom, you'll: (1) understand what you can achieve in a particular negotiation so you can set appropriate goals; (2) have several new tools and techniques to bring to the bargaining forum; and (3) consistently achieve significantly better results in most of your negotiations.

This book leans heavily toward the pragmatics of negotiating, identifying tactics you can use, while identifying some of the dirty tricks others may use on you. I provide lots of examples, many drawn from the thousands of transactions I have personally engineered and overseen as a sales pro, entrepreneur, corporate consultant, and attorney. Other practices have come from published sources, my clients, and my students.

Drawing inspiration from Aristotle and others, I believe when teaching, example is more effective than precept. You'll probably remember most of the Best Practices I'll identify, because they are brought to life through stories, case studies, and events that occurred. By contrast, some negotiation texts, programs, and gurus fail to hit the target: they're all theory or all practice, when reality requires the proper mixture of both.

Specifically, contributors to the field fall into one of two camps: (1) they are head-in-the-clouds theoreticians that are trying to invent and then overlay a grand intellectual model onto bargaining; or (2) they are out-of-the-trenches types who have war stories to tell, but are not effective at drawing out lessons that are applicable to others.

Like the proverbial tot whose only toy is a hammer, some negotiators see the world as a nail, to which that one tool or primary experience they've had is uniformly and punishingly misapplied.

Some pundits, for example, are former hostage negotiators. I think that's interesting work, but how pertinent is a guns-are-drawn, helicopters-are-circling atmosphere to striking a bargain on a car dealer's lot during a golden Sunday afternoon?

Other analysts have focused on union negotiations. The rules pertaining to collective bargaining are highly specialized. Often they can't be generalized to more informal sessions, which constitute the great majority of interactions we'll have when negotiating as businesspeople and consumers.

Contributors to the negotiation field suffer from some other problems as well. Academics are fond of negotiation schemes that seem "fair" and are based on a level playing field. I can't blame them, because fairness is an important value to me.

But those that assume there *is* a level playing field may fail to address the very real power differences between, say, a McDonald's executive and a small-fry business trying to sell toys to that behemoth for Happy Meals. With this prospective vendor, McDonald's has a huge advantage going into a bargaining session. Dismiss this fact, and you are placing doctrine and dogma over reality. What you might wish were the case simply is not.

Many textbooks on negotiation stress creating win-win outcomes. Instead of win-lose, which means that my gain is your loss, they emphasize no-lose outcomes for all. Instead of carving up a limited pie, the challenge is to bake a bigger pie, so we can both emerge with gigantic pieces, more than we ever expected or hoped for going in.

This can happen, providing negotiators are flexible, creative, and above all patient. But finding all three qualities in a negotiation counterpart is very unlikely (though later in the book I will share an example of a very creative and fruitful bargain that I was a party to when putting together a contract with an airline).

Speaking of "baking" better deals, we're going to turn next to a specific recipe for negotiating: six procedures that you'll want to use to make bargaining more palatable, enjoyable, and life- and career-sustaining.

Steps to a Successful Negotiation
THE FIRST STEP: MAKING SMALL TALK

"Have any problem finding the place?" is a typical ice-breaking phrase you'll hear people using when they get together for the first time. It isn't meant to elicit a blow-by-blow description of the harried trip someone had, but to get people to start talking, to make them share, to find some common ground.

This is really the first step in a negotiation, and some cultures invest a lot of time in taking it. For instance, when I was running a seminar at Hawaii Pacific University, several locals enlightened me about something they reverentially referred to as "talking story."

Talking story is much more than "Hi, how are you?" Actually, it is an elongated version of this phrase, and if you don't promote a reply that is lengthy, you simply aren't talking story correctly, I am led to understand.

"How are you?" is an invitation to talk about yourself, your relatives, current events, the weather, and anything else that comes to mind. If you fail to talk story, you can forget about getting to the heart of negotiations, because your negotiations will have no heart without this essential back-and-forth small talk.

I suppose the opposite of a Hawaiian's talking story is the New York minute—about three seconds, if that, to say hello and how are you? before plunging into deal points.

But even New Yorkers that play the negotiation game well know better than to push to hard too fast toward the details. They insert another step, too often missing from nearly everyone's bargaining sessions: signposting.

THE SECOND STEP: SIGNPOSTING

One of the most popular units in my training programs deals with building credibility.

It pays to be credible, because those that come across this way tend to be more persuasive. They're more often taken at their word, doubted less, and are given credit for knowing more than they do.

When we ask, "What makes someone credible?" three answers emerge: (1) trust, (2) expertise, and (3) dynamism.

To engineer a sense of trust and expertise, it is wise to seem *organized*. We know for a fact that organized communicators are more credible in various contexts, including negotiations.

I'm going to suggest you bring a list of objectives and deal points with you, to give an early sense of structure to the proceedings. This will enable you to *signpost*, to establish certain rules of the road.

"Here's what I was hoping we'd accomplish in our session today," you might begin. With this overture, you are accomplishing several things.

For one, you are asserting control over the agenda, which shows a serious intention to accomplish concrete results. This is a nice shift from the ice-breaking chitchat that you used to open communications a few minutes earlier. You are also setting standards for the session, setting the bar at a challenging but realistic level.

At this point, it is also wise to *negotiate the rules of negotiation*. This can involve setting time limits. For instance, you might say, "I'm planning on finalizing this today; does that sound reasonable to you?"

This can be followed with an all-important qualifying question: "Do you have the authority to accomplish this today?" (If not, your counterpart may be bargaining subject to a third party's approval, which means any presumed agreements are written in sand and can be blown away by someone else—something you need to know right away.)

If you get yesses in response, the time limit gives both of you something meaningful to shoot for. Bracketing the time available for bargaining produces a certain amount of *mutual urgency*. This can expedite agreement on minor points, which could otherwise be needless sticking points.

You can also agree to shut off your cell phones, thus limiting interruptions. Though this seems very minor, agreeing to do so makes it unlikely that a bogus "emergency back at the office" will derail your day, providing an alibi for one party to abruptly leave things at a standstill.

You can even set up a communication rule that says you'll take no more than one five-minute stretch break per hour, or that you'll pause every hour and a half for ten minutes.

These housekeeping details create miniagreements, and they can actually develop a sense of good will and forthrightness about the meat of the session to come.

With these details out of the way, you can go back to your list.

"OK, among the things I was hoping we'd discuss is the delivery time of the product. Specifically, when would you like that to happen?"

Then it is a matter of following your plan until all of the pertinent issues have been aired.

This brings us to the third step in the negotiation.

THE THIRD STEP:
PUTTING AN OFFER ON THE TABLE

Real estate agents frequently contact each another and say: "I have a client who may be interested in your listing. Can you tell me how flexible your seller is when it comes to price?"

It's really a trick question, because it might imply that the listing agent overpriced the property or that the sellers are unrealistic about what they are hoping to get.

However, instead of attacking the premise of the question, the best and most practical reply I've ever given is this one:

"How flexible are they? Well, let's find out. Bring us an offer!"

This is where the rubber meets the road. Once an offer for real estate is written and presented, negotiations are officially underway. A genuine offer empowers the seller to accept, to decline, or to counter the offer, remaking it into something she will accept.

So when we're discussing the anatomy of a negotiation transaction or the steps we take to get a negotiation on track and chugging in the right direction, we're speaking about either (1) making an offer or (2) getting your counterpart to volunteer one of his own.

There is a conflict of opinion regarding who wins more often: the person that is the first to offer, or the one that gets the other to offer first. Some believe in "dropping an anchor"—being the first person to talk price by stating what he's willing to do (which is typically much less than the other party expected to hear).

When I was selling a house for an elderly relative, a contractor offered me half of the price at which I had listed the property. That's dropping an anchor. His hope was that by lowballing, he would pull my price down to the depths, far lower than I would have gone without his tactic.

There is a lot of evidence to support the use of anchors, as I mention in Best Practice 2 of this book. When we hear a lowball offer, as we are recovering from shock, at least a part of us wonders if there is any way we can meet that price, while also worrying that if we don't meet it, will we lose the deal?

The other school of thought maintains that if we can get our counterparts to offer first, we might get lucky. They could start with a figure that is far higher than we had hoped, setting the stage for us to elevate our requirements to the stratosphere.

Both ploys can be effective, so there isn't a hard-and-fast rule regarding who needs to offer first. I would simply say that we won't go beyond preliminaries until we have some figure or deal points that we can discuss.

"Put something on the table!" is the adage that comes to mind. It is very much like writing a business letter or even a book. Until something goes onto the page, we have nothing. Once it is written down, there is some substance that can be edited, expanded, and otherwise enhanced.

As every writer can attest, it is always easier to edit than to write something new. So in a sense, both parties have done each other a favor by emitting an offer sooner rather than later.

THE FOURTH STEP: PRODUCING AGREEMENT

While we can't predict what will be acceptable to our counterparts, we can communicate in such a way as to nudge agreements along.

We do this by using techniques that are used in sales situations and by lawyers as they examine witnesses. I'm sure you're familiar with tie-downs, aren't you?

I've just used one. I made a statement: "I'm sure you're familiar with tie-downs." Then I checked back with a reflex-inducing question: "Aren't you?"

Let's say you're negotiating and you get stuck on a certain deal point. A tie-down can help: "Let's move on to another issue, and we can always return to this one later on, fair enough?"

When your counterpart agrees, you've just goosed the negotiations along.

What happens when you have reached a meeting of the minds on a deal point? "Good, we're agreed on this then. Delivery will be scheduled between Christmas and New Year's, right?"

The tie-down gives you real-time feedback, and it gets the other party to utter words of commitment. There are less formal opportunities to use tie-downs, as car dealers know.

"That model looks great in the silver blue, doesn't it?"

Most tie-downs follow the same pattern: make an affirmative statement and then check back for approval or acknowledgment. Harking back to the scheduling scenario, we could even try a negative form of the tie-down:

"We don't want delivery to spill over into the New Year, do we? That would jeopardize your ability to earn a tax credit in this calendar year, and that wouldn't be helpful, would it?"

Sometimes a simple "OK" will seal the deal: "So, it looks like our work is done here, and we have a deal, OK?"

Often your counterpart won't need a tie-down. He'll close a deal or a deal point on his own.

"Well, that seems fair. Sign me up!"

Still, it's useful to have tie-downs in your arsenal so you can engineer assent on the spot, at will.

But once you have your commitments, you're still not through with the full negotiation sequence. Two vital steps remain.

THE FIFTH STEP:
CONFIRMING YOUR RESPECTIVE COMMITMENTS
Every smart seller knows that getting someone to utter words of agreement is crucial, but you still have a way to go until you reach the end zone, score a touchdown, and then earn the extra points.

You need to *bolster* the agreement at which you've apparently arrived. This involves *repeating* the main deal points and ferreting out any latent questions or points of resistance or misunderstanding.

"Great, just so we're clear," you begin, "we're going to A, B, C, D, and E, and we're agreeing to a delivery date between Christmas and New Year's. The total price including taxes and delivery will be $15,249, and payment will be on delivery, right? Very good. Do you have any questions?"

THE SIXTH STEP: ACTION AND IMPLEMENTATION

As we've already seen, a Best Practice in Negotiation is appreciating that the deal isn't made until the money is paid. Just because we have used words of agreement, have shaken hands, and are basking in the glow of our bargaining achievement doesn't mean the negotiation is finished.

Action must be taken, and specifics need to be implemented.

For example, as a consultant, in the interest of improving my cash flow and creating a sense of transparency about my expenses, I'll ask my client to purchase my airline tickets, secure hotels, and have these billed directly to the client.

My contractual "performance" consists of many steps, including off-site preparation of training material, program design, coordination with the client, and, when called for, development of new techniques for selling, servicing, and negotiating. But there is an on-site component as well at their offices and sometimes at hotels and resorts, if I am retained to deliver a speech or a seminar.

The clients pay, which is their contractual performance—their side of the bargain. And I plan, customize, speak, and consult to earn their pay.

But the deal isn't really made in the Dun & Bradstreet sense until they signal their commitment.

Purchasing my airline tickets and securing my hotel accommodations signals that they are moving ahead with the remainder of the program.

These steps need to be taken, but a traditional way of handling flight and rooms is for a consultant or speaker to advance the costs and bill the client for them later. This ties up the consultant's credit lines and amounts to making a loan to the client. It shifts too much risk to my company in the event that my employers are a "slow-pay," taking many months to pay invoices. In a tough economy, they could even declare bankruptcy, leaving me with a large unpaid tab.

So I accomplish many things by getting travel costs paid up front. Perhaps the most significant is *getting my counterparts to take immediate action implementing our agreement.*

Again, without action and implementation, your negotiation isn't complete. You need to move through all six steps of the anatomy of a negotiation to bring deals to fruition.

We could invest a lot more time and pages in elaborating what occurs during the negotiation sequence. However, I think this detailing is best left to the 77 Best Practices that I'm going to enumerate next.

I've argued with myself repeatedly about whether there is an optimal organizing principle through which to present these do's and don'ts. But the typical structural precepts simply don't seem to apply as they did in presenting the material in this chapter. Here we used a temporal format, starting with step 1 and moving through step 6. The 77 tips do not follow a given time sequence. Often several will come into play simultaneously. As someone is "dropping the anchor," he is also trying to get you to "negotiate against yourself" by inducing you to reduce your demands before he has conceded anything.

In the cut-and-thrust of bargaining, you'll need to determine for yourself whether and how to deal with these tactics: both in sequence, dealing with one alone, or ignoring both and proceeding with your game plan.

You'll find the Best Practices are organized roughly by title, topic, and strategy. But they aren't collected and presented in divisions or under various headings. This lack of prioritizing is actually liberating for the reader, because you can skip around without losing a feeling of continuity.

Feel free to cherry-pick the ripest and plumpest topics for you at the moment. Reread the practices several times over, and you'll probably get more from them with each pass.

A final observation: Instead of 77, there may be 177 or even 1,777 Best Practices in Negotiation. For creative and practical purposes, I had to aim at a figure and stop somewhere.

The Best Practices detailed here are the ones I have judged to be the best, and I take full responsibility for their inclusion. I didn't answer to a committee, nor did I take a vote among negotiation practitioners or pundits. I used my judgment, experience, and training in enumerating them.

Many are 100 percent original. I invented them, or at least I am the first to articulate them for others. In some cases they are the best by default: they fill a vacuum, providing a winning strategy where none existed or where none was widely shared before.

A few gambits may already be familiar to you.

You might call these "consensus Best Practices," since they recur in the literature.

They're tried and true, yet because they are often so widely known, they fail to work their magic when both parties to a negotiation are familiar with them.

I'll touch on this in the pages to come.

For now, buckle up and enjoy the ride. Please let me know how these techniques work for you. And good luck!

Chapter 3

77 Best Practices In Negotiation

. . . .

Best Practice 1
It Isn't What You Charge,
It's What You Earn

I'm a huge fan of dollar stores. Yesterday, for example, it occurred to me I could use some sink stoppers—you know, those simple rubber plugs. I thought about hitting a hardware store, where I figured I'd probably have to pay about $2.99 each.

Instead I drove to a dollar store, which was even closer, and they had them. While I was there, I picked up a can opener and a few other necessities, which would have set me back three, four, or five times as much money at other outlets.

At roughly a buck an item, this chain and similar ones have revolutionized retailing, while earning tidy profits.

They're focusing on what people want to pay, not on what they'd like to charge.

Along with tremendous inventory sourcing and some other trade skills, this is the real entrepreneurial lesson of dollar stores.

Negotiators usually ask the wrong questions when they prepare to transact. One of them is, *"How much can I charge?"*

Maximizing our gains is only rational, right? Isn't this what we've been taught in Capitalism 101?

Generally this is true, but in retailing, for example, the traditional formula still applies. Profits result from margin over costs times product turns. Dollar stores may be earning pennies on each item that leaves the store, but they're selling a lot of items.

If this company decided to become the $1.99 store, their product turns would diminish probably by much more than half, consequently shrinking profits.

For a very long time in my consulting practice, I took pride in how much money I charged. That's right: if I had been an automobile, I would have been well into the high range of luxury class.

To me, price signaled value. "I'm worth it!" was the unspoken motto. Indeed, when one prospect balked at my fees, he said, "Why, the average consultant charges only X dollars a day."

You know what I said: "I charge what I do because I'm *not average!*"

But I *was* arrogant, and when a world of competitors entered the scene, ushered in by the Internet, I had to rethink my positioning. No longer was it self-evident that I was the best provider of keynote speeches, seminars, and consulting in customer service, negotiation, communication skills, and telephone selling.

The message I was hearing was clear: adjust to charging what people want to pay, not what you want to charge—that is, if you prefer to stay busy plying your trade.

The primary gain in business and in negotiations is achieving a profit, not in maintaining and justifying premium pricing.

That's my dollar's worth of advice for the day!

. . . .

Best Practice 2
Drop Your Anchor, Matey!

Bob needed to move two pianos from one residence to the next, and if you've ever had to move one yourself, you quickly realize this isn't something you can do solo.

Experts have to carefully dissemble grand pianos and then reassemble them at the end of the line. Uprights are easier to shuttle, but they probably weigh the same as locomotives.

And that word is fitting, because your motives must be loco, a little crazy, to schlep a piano, let alone two of them.

There aren't that many experts in piano moving, so they can and do charge hefty fees. Bob had a tiny budget, but he did have some negotiation savvy.

He phoned a few piano stores and found out which mover they used, and he even teased out what they paid this firm. Armed with this information, which suggested the price would be about $360, Bob contacted the movers told them his budget was $200. Then he added that he had a washer and dryer that he wanted them to move as well.

Those items would put the price at $400 or more, they replied. After some give-and-take, Bob got them to accept $265 for everything. By sinking his anchor before they had a chance to recite their prices, he did well.

Mentioning a superlow budget figure has the effect of making your counterpart ask himself, "Could I possibly do it for this amount?"

Divulging a budget constraint right away makes you sound credible, as if you've taken time to devise a top-dollar amount you can pay. Compare this to how many people negotiate.

"How much would it cost to move two pianos, one a baby grand, plus a washer and dryer, from here to there?"

"That would be about $450."

"Ooh, that's steep. Could you do it for $200?"

"Get outta here and never darken my doorstep again!"

You have to admit, it seems as if we're insulting someone by countering their $450 with $200, correct?

So the timing of the anchor is critical, and it's called an anchor because it narrows your movement in what would be a tumultuous sea of negotiation.

You and your counterpart are only going to drift so far from the anchor point.

Here is your Best Practice in Negotiation learning point: Drop your anchor first, or your counteroffer will probably get torpedoed!

. . . .

Best Practice 3
Is It a Trick?

Jack wanted to sell his kayak, so he listed it online and got a few inquiries.

One couple came over with a truck—a good sign—but the wife criticized the item in a voice that could be heard down the block.

Jack had Googled her name before she arrived. He expected divalike behavior, having discovered that she is an actress in regional theater productions.

Examining the kayak, she bellowed to her husband, "I thought it would be LARGER!" He was standing right next to her.

Was her loud lament a negotiation trick or a heartfelt expression of chagrin? Did she hope that by lambasting the item, she would lower the price?

Jack thought so, and he purposely elected not to react.

Imperiously, she departed with her spouse. About three minutes later, she returned, rang the bell, strode up to Jack, and made an offer that was a third lower than the asking price.

Another ploy?

"Definitely," says Jack, no stranger to this bargaining dance.

"Walking away was her big move," he explained. "It's taught as a tactic in negotiation books. She mistakenly thought I would follow her out the door, as if I were running a bazaar!"

Another couple expressed interest, but canceled an appointment an hour after the agreed meeting time. Phoning, one of the partners said she wanted to photograph the kayak to show to her husband.

Jack tentatively set a meeting for that purpose, but then recanted, explaining that it made no sense to show it if no offer could be made at the same time.

Were her belated cancellation and photo request tricks?

"If you're serious about buying, you cut to the chase. You don't add needless steps to the process," Jake mused.

Expect tricks, gambits, lowball offers, and delays. Like battles, few negotiations turn out exactly as planned.

As for Best Practices in Negotiation, you can count on this rule: *if you think it is a trick or a ploy, you're probably right.*

Jack did sell his kayak to the second couple after establishing this ground rule to lend seriousness to the process: "When you come to see it, bring cash and a truck."

They brought the cash.

"Good enough!" Jack smiled.

. . . .

Best Practice 4
Don't Give Away the Store

In this economy, customers are so risk-averse that selling is becoming more and more painful.

They're price-shopping like crazy, procrastinating, paying later, ducking out of deals, and renegotiating terms without shame.

For instance, Larry sells tools. One of his customers paid for its order by check but purposely subtracted the shipping fee—about $180—claiming Larry never mentioned it.

"That's ridiculous!" he exclaimed after hearing how they altered the deal after the fact. "It's written all over our brochures that they pay shipping," he added, as he paced the sales room in disgust.

His commission was reduced by the same amount, $180, as if he had thrown it into the deal.

It can be difficult to distinguish between outright fraud, where customers are lying, and relentless grinding of vendors to achieve better deals. During previous recessions and times of tight money, I've used and advocated using satisfaction guarantees to bolster sales.

"If you're not happy, you don't pay!" is the most open-ended guarantee you can offer. But if you do, are *you* accepting too much risk?

I believe you are, because happiness is subjective. Buyers can wake up one day and decide they aren't completely pleased and return your product, or, worse, they can enjoy the benefits of your service without having to pay the tab.

In good economies, this is less of a threat to your peace of mind and profits. Marginally satisfied clients may still choose to pay, because they have the money and want to avoid a potential confrontation, even if only being asked, "Why?"

But in tough times, they don't have many discretionary dollars, and several needs are lobbying for the same scarce money at a given time. It seems ideal to try but not buy, from the standpoint of reducing their risks.

If you're selling Mrs. Fields' cookies in a mall, you can crumble a few of your products and offer free tastings. Or if you operate a winery, you can dispense a sample in hopes of generating sufficient business to cover costs.

But what if you're in the advertising or public-relations field and you're asked to pitch a prospect on a campaign? Should you develop a theme and a conceptualization of the overall project on spec, trusting that the listeners won't rip off your ideas?

If you're a call center, should you study the prospect's needs, write a presentation, train staff, and make test calls—all for free—hoping your success, if any, will eventuate in a profitable relationship?

In a word, no.

Amateurs, interns, and the desperate work for nothing, hoping that nothing will turn into something. That's like starting with zero, in arithmetic, and multiplying it by 100. The result is still zero.

Let me offer this mantra, which you should repeat over and over:

Clients must pay something!

For example, a school board candidate came to me for two speeches: a stump talk that she could use repeatedly, and an acceptance speech. She sent me her rough draft.

I quoted my fee, which she said was beyond her budget, because she was not accepting campaign contributions. I gave her an alternative. I said I would edit her talk and make some recommendations for rewriting it.

Well, I ended up rewriting it, because that was easier and more productive for both of us. But I was still paid for my ministrations.

Her risks were moderated, and I took on the risk of doing too much relative to the compensation. Still, we fashioned a win-win relationship.

Sometimes sprinkling bread upon the water makes sense.

A bankruptcy lawyer offers a free thirty-minute initial consultation for consumers. Another attorney and I were discussing marketing tactics, and he mentioned her, because her office is in the same building.

"She has a line of clients out the door," he noted with admiration.

Naturally, I attributed part of that apparent success to the economy. Millions are in financial distress, so helping folks battle insolvency by fending off swarms of swooping creditors can be big business.

Yet you also have to ask, to what extent is the free initial consultation an attraction? Would a charge for the first meeting thin the standing-room-only crowds?

I believe the freebie is necessary, because it serves both parties, especially the attorney.

1. She can quickly determine whether the prospective client qualifies. Maybe a recent filing precludes a current one.

2. She can ask a few questions to learn which bankruptcy chapter the person qualifies for: 7 or 13.

3. She can determine if there is an impending garnishment of wages, a tax lien, or an auto repossession that requires a swift filing at the earliest possible moment.

4. She can learn if the client can afford to retain legal counsel.

5. She can sense if the client will be too much of a headache or too demanding (which should be avoided).

All these things and more need to be learned and assessed. So the free meeting really serves the information provider. In this sense, it is neither free nor gratuitous; it is essential. I have no problem with this type of business enticement. Inevitably the lawyer will dispense a modicum of helpful advice gratis. It is practically unavoidable. I don't see this as a loss, but as part of a larger win-win scenario for the parties. Consider it an investment in the relationship.

I do find *free* inappropriate, offensive, and as profane as a four-letter word when:

1. The information being sought is valuable and usually dispensed carefully and thoughtfully in the ordinary course of a professional's practice. The client who gets thirty minutes has no right to insist that the lawyer prepare the bankruptcy filing, which involves considerable time and expertise, for free as well.

2. Other people typically pay for this information. Lots of lawyers will offer a free initial consultation. It's somewhat commonplace. But if someone comes to me to critique a sales or service script, then he has to pay. I know of no consultant that does this for free. It isn't a giveaway.

3. The freebie seeker can afford to pay the going rate, yet wants to get something for nothing.

4. The information provider is deceived into believing that *free* will become *fee*. Ad agencies, graphic designers, writers, and lots of creatives are victimized. They're asked to submit proposals on spec, addressing the very task the client wants to accomplish. Ad agencies will be asked to pitch their concept for theme development for a new shopping mall. In principle, if their proposed campaign is attractive, their bid will be chosen. In reality, the client is simply brain picking, with no intention to retain an agency, thinking it will combine or disguise the contributions and use them for free.

5. Free service is requested or demanded without a corresponding duty on the part of the freebie seeker. For example, if you go to the cosmetics counter at a department store, you may be treated to a goodie bag

free with your purchase. That's fair, but free without purchase or *any* obligation to reciprocate is patently unfair. More to the point, it is economically unsustainable. The lawyer, consultant, writer, artist, or worker of any kind that gives away her talents cannot invest the same hours and days in paying work. *Free* precludes *fee* instead of leading to it.

To be asked to do your work for nothing is unrealistic and insulting.

Don't be conned into doing it. There is no future in giving away the store. We have to be extra diligent in avoiding customers that prompt us to do so.

. . . .

Best Practice 5
Raise Your Prices

Would you agree with the following proposition? *The longer it takes you to sell something, the more expensive it becomes for you to sell it.*

Economists refer to this added expense as a *transaction cost.* Your time and effort, as well as advertising and staging of the item for sale, all require money or money's equivalents in know-how, time, and elbow grease.

Therefore the more time passes in a negotiation, the less we're netting out from our sale, even if the price never changes. If I start dickering at a $100 price, but it costs me $50 in clock time to collect that $100, I really brought in $50, correct?

When I bought my first home, the seller was working on an extended contract in the oil fields of the Middle East. I submitted a relatively low offer and accompanied it with this statement, which I hoped his agent would convey to him:

"We're genuinely interested, but it's our first house, and we can't afford more. This will be our best and only offer. Let's save everyone some time and needless back-and-forth communication."

The agent cut her commission a little—which she could afford to do, because it was her listing—and we moved in.

The seller understood transaction costs. What good would it have done him to have waited and waited for a few thousand more?

You're with me so far, but now let's take a logical leap, shall we?

If time is money, then a fast deal is worth more than a delayed deal. Consequently, the price of an item should go up with the passage of time, shouldn't it? If it costs me more to sell it to you, you should pay me more for it, yes?

I was trying to sell another house. There was only one genuine buyer that presented himself through an agent, but his agent's strategy was to wait to submit an offer until I reduced the price. Deciding I needed a way to smoke out his interest, I raised the price by $100,000.

I knew that the multiple listing service would automatically notify the agent, so I didn't need to do anything but wait for the response.

The buyer and his agent were flummoxed by my gambit, but his agent contacted me right away. Within twenty-four hours, the buyer made a written offer, fearing he'd have to pay a hundred grand more for the place.

They don't teach you this strategy in real estate school.

But it's rational, if you think about it.

Consider telling prospective clients, "If you give me a quick order, this keeps my costs low, and I can pass on the savings. If you delay or I'm forced to follow up relentlessly, then it costs me more, and I'll need to pass the costs along to you. Make sense?"

This will tell you where you stand, separating the serious from the frivolous, and you'll be telling the truth.

Many negotiators foolishly believe that costs will plummet if they play a waiting game or play hard to get.

Show them it doesn't necessarily work that way!

. . . .

Best Practice 6
Leave a Little Extra on the Table

The other day a server at a museum café forgot to bring my beverage after four requests.

Finally, she delivered it with an apology, and made the gesture of not charging me for it, which was some consolation. Still it would have been nice to have used it for the purpose of enabling my food to more smoothly make its downward passage.

Tip time came around. I had to do some calculations. Putting the tardy drink aside, was she pleasant and helpful? Yes.

Did she seem to be the only person on the floor? Yes again. Have to have some empathy for that.

Had she been flawless, she would have earned $4.50. The late drink after four requests would have made that plummet to $1.50. But her gesture earns at least another buck and a half back. We're up to $3.

I left $4, adding an extra buck at the last minute. This was only fifty cents shy of a tip for flawless service. But I left the buck as an investment in the future, a way of preserving good will so our rapport could reset.

In negotiation terminology, I left some money on the table—a little bit more than I had to do—as my gesture.

You'll find ample chances to do this well beyond the realm of restaurants. Let's say you're about to rent an apartment, and the landlord wants $200 above your price point.

Because it's the off-season where you are renting, you could hold out for the full concession, a price break of $200. But what if he knocks off $150, leaving a $50 upgrade over what you hoped to spend? Will you say, "OK?"

You have to ask, is it worth the hassle to save another $50 a month? Would you lose more in goodwill by insisting on it? Haven't you done well enough in this negotiation by shearing off $150 monthly?

Moreover, by playing hardball, do you run the risk that the landlord will simply wash his hands of you if you don't concede the issue?

If you want to be cynical, you could see what I'm doing as less than angelic. Even pool hustlers won't completely run the table, revealing their actual abilities. They purposely miss a shot, showing a little vulnerability. That way, when it comes time to rack 'em up again, they won't find themselves playing alone.

. . . .

Best Practice 7
"How Much Do You Charge?"

There are three T's in any negotiation: *text*, *tone*, and *timing*, which refer to *what* someone says, *how* they say it, and *when* they say it.

Think of the three T's as a rope with fibers that spiral around and around, each separate from yet supporting one another.

Just this morning I received an email from someone interested in my writing and editing services. He asked, "What do you charge?"

Now that's a completely fair question. But the timing of it is crucial.

If, for instance, it is asked at the end of a meaningful conversation, where a product or service has been explained and offered, then addressing price is completely appropriate and intelligent. By asking how much we charge, our counterpart is expressing a buying signal, and is ready to calibrate price to promised performance.

"That seems reasonable" is what we hope the listener will conclude.

But what if price is broached before you've had a meaningful conversation, as it was in the email I received?

The rope I mentioned above has just become a noose dangling before you, a trap for the unwary, a threat. You do not want to step into it. Several points:

1. It could be a competitor doing a little benchmarking or spy work.

2. It could be a competitor's client that wants to keep your foe honest or find some fodder for extracting concessions in a negotiation.

3. If it is a genuine prospect, he or she is simply asking a good question, but completely out of order.

4. If you answer it, you'll err, because you cannot quote in a vacuum. "How much do I charge *for what?*" is the true question.

5. Answering it with a figure allows the inquirer to make his own judgment based on budgetary factors that may simply not apply. For instance, if you ask me what I charge for an hour of my time, the reply could be as high as $10,000 or $15,000, if you want me in Europe or Brazil delivering a keynote speech to an important audience. To write or edit a speech for someone else might be significantly less pricey, if only because I don't have to invest a business week in traveling to and from a distant locale so I can deliver that dynamic one-hour talk.

Be prepared to follow the "negative," that is, price, with a "positive," a statement taking the sting out of your quotation:

"The fee for your speech will be only $15,000, which is very reasonable considering my investment of more than a week's time in preparation and travel, substantial customizing and expertise, and my competitors' fees, which are generally 25–50 percent higher."

Remember this Best Practice in Negotiation: as a rule, *never state a price out of context*. If you do, I assure you it will sound too expensive.

. . . .

Best Practice 8
Distinguish Buying from Lying

One of the most crucial skills you can develop as a negotiator is determining when someone is sending you a false signal of interest in your offer.

Often you'll hear people say, as I did the other day, "I'm going to sleep on it."

I phoned him back the next day to see if he'd improve his offer. Again he said he'd sleep on it, at which point I quipped, "That's what you said yesterday. By now I'd think you're very well rested."

Another person remarked, "I'll call around, and if I find a buyer, I'll let you know."

Encouraging signs, or brush-offs?

Amateurs would reply, "Well, at least they didn't say no!" Actually, it's worse. A no tells you something specific: either change your offer or find someone else. A maybe or a stall can waste your time, raising false hopes.

I was just reading a blog for attorneys. The author described a phone conversation she had with an attorney's assistant, who happened to be his wife:

"The attorney's wife said she would talk to her husband. I knew right then and there that she was not happy with the price. How did I know? Because if she had been interested in my services, she would have asked me questions and sought out details of how my work would be performed. Instead, as soon as she learned my price, she dropped the ball and found an excuse to get off the phone. These are things you need to look for when marketing your service business."

I couldn't agree more.

This blogger went on to say that just to be sure, she emailed the law firm about a week later and received a terse reply that her prices were too high, which proved that she was being jettisoned over the phone.

You need to be able to separate the serious from the frivolous, buying signals from lying signals. The earlier you can detect the difference, the better off you'll be, and the more profitable and effective.

. . . .

Best Practice 9
A Rough Courtship Signals a Rougher Marriage

When negotiating, we can wrongly believe we're the Roman legions, able to march into distant lands and conquer, bending inferiors to our will. We feel omnipotent.

With proven techniques deployed here and there, we can deftly cut through resistance and accomplish nearly any objective.

Sometimes we do prevail, and bargaining feels exactly like that.

I recall the campaign of conquest that launched my successful seminar business. Having designed a simple but compelling conversation starter, I persuaded about fifty key partners from Hawaii to New York to sponsor my training programs, a circuit of classes, which I developed and traveled in about eighteen months. From that beginning came top-tier speaking opportunities, requests to write best-selling books, and more clients.

To this day, I recall the very few prospects that declined, the ones who defied my ostensible success and remained steadfastly outside of my orbit. At the time, I was perplexed that they held out. It offended me, which tells you how much I took success for granted.

But now I see one important fact of negotiation that eluded me: we don't control nearly as many of the variables in bargaining as we think. When people decline, or a deal falls through, or we meet with unusual resistance, it is a good time to appreciate that we simply aren't right for everyone or every situation.

Step back, and contemplate matters. Call a time out. Regroup.

An old adage from love literature comes to mind: a tempestuous courtship means a tempestuous relationship will follow.

Let's say it takes you an unusually long time to open discussions and then to sell a client. You might think that the elongated preliminaries aired all the issues and answered every question, and now the sailing will be smooth.

Not so.

That reluctant client, whose incessant concerns you tried to dispatch with the verbal equivalent of whack-a-mole, hasn't reformed or changed his paranoid pattern of thinking. He is very likely to foster yet more worries after you think the deal is done, and to suffer from buyer's remorse.

At minimum, this will require oodles of postsale customer service and hand-holding, which are costly to you, preventing you from romancing better partners. And if a client's regret is strong enough, he may stiff you, refusing to pay for the goods or services you have already tendered.

Compared to customer service, collections efforts are even more vexing. Looking back, you'll wish you never wasted your time with such a loser.

"How did it come to this?" you'll ask yourself at three in the morning, over a glass of milk or something stronger.

The other day and I came across the movie *A Bridge Too Far*, about a World War II battle of attrition, a bog that should have been avoided.

If you're finding a negotiation partner too resistant, especially early in your discussions, take that as a cue to cease activity, to end your session as quickly yet as politely as possible.

Don't push your way to a victory that could mire you in defeat.

. . . .

Best Practice 10
Offer a Buy-Now Price

The savvy negotiator can learn a thing or two by studying eBay.

Though I've purchased only a couple of items at the auction site, one aspect of it is worth emulating when you are setting your sales prices for goods or services.

It's the *buy-now price.*

Typically, sellers offer two options to you. One is to enter the scheduled bidding, taking a chance that you can outlast and outspend any number of suitors. The other is easier yet more expensive: to seize the buy-now price, a fixed figure that will save you time and assure you of emerging with the product you're pursuing.

Instead of setting a higher buy-now price, for many negotiators I suggest setting it *lower.* That way we pass on savings to those that will make faster buying decisions. Implicitly, we do something else that is pretty clever. *We put a high price tag on haggling.*

Let's say someone wants to retain a speaker for a conference scheduled three months from now. She can offer them this deal: "Buy now, and my fee will only be $7,500. Wait thirty days, and the price will rise to $8,500. Procrastinate for 45 days or more from the inception of our discussions, and your fee will be $10,000, *if the date is still available.*"

This might seem punitive, and in a way it is. People are punished for stringing sellers along, for trying to comparison-shop, and then for grinding them on price.

Apart from eBay, is there any precedent for doing this? Absolutely, and it's one that every traveler knows only too well: if you can book your flight thirty days or more in advance—that is, buy now—you'll probably be able to qualify for supersaver fares, usually the very cheapest available. As you get closer to your departure date, fares jump into the stratosphere.

Airlines enable us to hold an itinerary for a very short time without committing. It may be 24, 48, 72, or slightly more hours, but we have to pull the trigger very quickly to hit the lowest price target. And until we pay, the fare isn't guaranteed, nor is our favorite seat.

What I like about a buy-now price is that it officially reverses the thinking of many negotiators: "If I simply wait, he'll drop his price."

A buy-now price says: wait and pay more, or risk being shut out of purchasing altogether.

As far as I'm concerned, this is not only a good idea. It qualifies as a Best Practice.

. . . .

Best Practice 11
Win or Lose, You Win!

Sometimes I question the wisdom of my colleagues in the negotiation training field. I wonder if they have personally engaged in enough bargaining sessions, and if they have, are they current on today's marketplace dynamics?

For instance, in my recent seminar at UCLA Extension, we were discussing a case study of workplace negotiation. I've used this case for three years, and as time passes, the strategies employed seem to change dramatically.

The other day, for instance, I found bargaining pairs were unusually conciliatory toward each other. A mere twenty-four months ago, their counterparts were at each others' throats.

Why the change? To paraphrase a presidential candidate, "It's the economy, dummy!"

Today subordinates bite their lips a hundred times before confronting their superiors, lest they antagonize and alienate them, and in doing so elevate themselves to the top of the expendables list for the next spate of layoffs.

Fighting unfairness, poor treatment, pay cuts, and miscellaneous insults and injuries is potentially problematic. But there are times when increasing your willingness to confront makes sense.

You might recall the movie *Raging Bull*, about boxer Jake LaMotta. At one point, his brother, who is also his professional manager, explains the logic of accepting a bout. Because the foe is ranked higher than LaMotta, his sibling explains: "Take the fight because if you win, you win, and if you lose, you win!"

Certain negotiations are like that fight. They present opportunities to give you exposure, to sharpen your skills, and even if they result in a nominal loss, they constitute a net gain for you.

Interviewing for jobs comes to mind. The more you interview, even for less desirable positions, or for those that are beyond your potential to perform, the better you'll get at this necessary skill.

When I was a sales manager with Time-Life, one of my reps loved to go on interviews and would report his triumphs to me. Mind you, he had no intention of bolting from our company. He just wanted to compare us to others and to enhance his interviewing skills.

The test of his prowess was the job offers he elicited, and there were quite a few. I indulged him because his briefings enabled me to do some competitive benchmarking, to sense where Time-Life needed to be in order to remain competitive in recruiting and retaining employees.

I suppose if this seller did find a disproportionately better job, he would have taken it, but irrespective of the outcome, if he won, he won, and if he lost and no job was offered, he still won.

You can do the same, by accepting nearly every opportunity to bargain. You'll find, the less you *must* win, the more you will gain.

. . . .

Best Practice 12
Ask, "How Did You Arrive at That Price?"

Boarding an elevator with my client, I shocked him when he asked me if I was busy with consulting work.

"Right now," I replied, "I'd buy back my time at $2,500 a day," which was what I was charging his firm at the time.

Demand for my services was so strong that my rate had jumped to $3,500–$4,500, so I was being absolutely truthful. When we inked our deal, he locked in a bargain.

Over time I've learned to support my pricing with strong rationales. Sometimes this even takes the form of written documentation.

For instance, I was selling a barbecue on Craigslist, and I indicated that it was like new. Then I added links showing what new barbecues of its manufacture were selling for, which was three times as much.

Thus I justified the price by saying that people would have to spend three times as much to get a comparable item, and I proved it. This saved a lot of time in haggling and helped to buttress my price.

But most negotiators don't do what I do. They recite certain prices and never explain them. If you want to get them to discount, you need to ask: *"How did you arrive at that price?"*

Often you'll find they pulled it out of thin air, though they won't say as much. They'll hem and haw, or they might mention that they paid close to that amount for the product.

No matter what they say, they have offered information you can explore further and politely challenge.

For instance, if you're buying a used car from a private party and they respond that they found the price in the Kelley Blue Book, you could say, "That's great. When did you consult the Blue Book, and do you have a printout?"

The fact is that KBB is constantly being updated, so this quarter's prices certainly won't be next quarter's. Models change and become obsolete, fuel prices fluctuate, and recalls are publicized, all of which impact the value of cars. Plus, Kelley adds value for certain equipment and deducts for other things, such as body damage and higher than average mileage.

All of these variables offer opportunities for discounting. You can consult Kelley together, in the here and now, plugging in the pertinent data. This can yield a figure you can both agree to.

Getting beyond the stated price into the reasoning that supports it is a technique that comes out of the.

It is definitely a Best Practice in Negotiation because it enables bargainers to avoid deadlocking over price. Instead of endlessly saying, "I need X price" and hearing back, "But I'm only willing to pay Y price," remember to ask, "How did you arrive at that figure?"

· · · · · · · · · · · · · ·

Best Practice 13
When Does Hard Haggling Help or Hurt?

There is a cigar-chomping, hard-haggling negotiator that we've seen characterized in movies and comic books and novels.

A bully, really, he makes the rules and breaks them at will, riding roughshod over everything and everyone in his way. A bully, really, he gets what he wants and is the last person standing when the fur stops flying.

Do these people exist, and are their techniques truly effective?

Yes, they exist, and they can be quite effective, providing they are negotiating for *products* and not for *services*.

This distinction is crucial.

Let's say Blustery Bill needs to buy some copper wire. Typically, this is a commodity, and assuming numerous suppliers have it in stock in the required gauges, BB can take his pick.

"It's only a matter of price and payment terms," he says with cynical conclusiveness. He'll buy, at long last, from the source that will buckle the most to his demands.

BB doesn't care if he is liked, because copper wire is copper wire, period. Bluster and bullying pay off time and again in bare-bones deals.

But let's say BB is negotiating to hire a sales assistant. In this case, he's bargaining for the delivery of services, which are anything but standardized commodities.

If BB beats up every job candidate in interviews, he's very unlikely to find someone that wants to work with him. Volition, free will, and desire can't be dictated.

In almost every scenario in which performance is determined in at least equal measure by the performer, BB will lose valuable cooperation. Thus, his "best practice" in purchasing copper wire becomes a worst practice when purchasing services.

Learning point: be flexible, and select a negotiation style that is suitable to the circumstances.

. . . .

Best Practice 14
The Nibbler versus the Camel

There are a number of purportedly scientific ways to study negotiation.

One of them is mathematical modeling of decision making, also known as *game theory*. This area attempts to quantify the probabilities that A will or will not do X in his bargaining with B. Game theory was one of the tools used during the Cold War to work through the scenarios in which the superpowers would or would not engage in a nuclear attack.

The problem with scientific approaches is that they don't adequately measure or predict such human motivations as greed and disgust, nor do they fully take into account the histories of the negotiators. I like to point out the quite unpredictable moves people make when they are engaged in a "nibbling" encounter.

Nibbling, a term coined by negotiation pundit Herb Cohen, is trying to improve a deal by getting an extra morsel, often as transactions are culminating. One example is a man shopping for a business suit. After he has tried it on, and it has been chalked and pinned by the tailor, the customer asks which shirt and tie the salesperson would recommend to complement the ensemble.

Enthusiastically, the clerk returns with a crisp shirt and power tie. The customer removes the jacket and pants and asks, "If I buy the suit, will you throw in the shirt and tie?"

At this point the customer seems to be in control. The seller and his tailor have an ego involvement in writing up the order. As a percentage of the overall purchase, the shirt and tie are not much extra, at least computed at cost to the store.

All the seller has to do is cut his commission a little, and he has an order. But will he buckle?

Nibbling advocates predict he will, at least often enough to make the gambit a successful one for the customer. They say greed will conquer disgust.

Not necessarily.

One perspective says the way people treat you is only remotely a reflection of you. More likely, it will mirror how they have been handled by the people who arrived on the scene before you did.

If the clerk is already disgusted with window shoppers and other time wasters before you nibbled, to mix the metaphor, your behavior could be the last straw, breaking the camel's back.

On the ground of "principle," he may reject your nibble and force you to take the suit or leave it, which you may find an unsettling ultimatum. You lose the suit, he loses a sale of any kind, and you both lose the time you invested and feel emotionally ruffled.

Negotiation isn't a simple matter of outcomes and seeming to get a good deal, denominated in dollars. It also involves human transaction costs and benefits.

If you seek royal treatment in a clothing store, does it make sense to behave like a beggar?

Nibbling seems to concern itself with crumbs. This hardly seems like a profitable enterprise, except for those that are merely pretending to be interested in a meal.

. . . .

Best Practice 15
The Deal Isn't Made Until the Money Is Paid

One of my most puzzling negotiations involved what at the outset seemed to be a simple matter of confirming some consulting dates.

A prior client contacted me by phone and left a voicemail expressing interest in a customized seminar. I phoned back promptly, and we had a very upbeat and detailed chat, during which I indicated my calendar was better for booking sooner than later.

My follow-up email offered a set of dates about five weeks away, and I awaited an overnight check to secure the time slot. A week later, the check still hadn't come, forcing me to write an email expressing concern, which didn't receive a response either.

Not appreciating business mysteries, I phoned within a few hours of sending that email. I was told that there was a split of opinion at the client's company about the dates I suggested, which were actually dates my client had selected.

Again, we had a nice conversation, and I was assured I'd have my confirmation the next day, which also came and went in silence. Finally, after yet another phone call, I got an email requesting dates two months into the future, which I supplied promptly, also requesting confirmation.

But that led to more silence.

Whom was I to believe: the positive and definite phone person or the elusive email enigma?

This is not an easy question to answer. Just as some folks are easier to sell through one medium versus another, there are also people that are better at dissimulation by phone or email.

Complicating the interpretive process is the fact that many people are awful writers and know it, so their missives sound stiff and strategic, or they avoid putting paws to keyboard altogether, fearing they'll make an indelible mistake or embarrass themselves. In short, we could wait forever for them to write a responsive email.

Sometimes people suffer from phone fear, a sort of situational shyness or performance anxiety that makes them sound evasive or overly cautious. The human voice isn't a reliable conveyor of all the facts we'd like to know at a given time.

We just can't say, "Trust email, because if you get a commitment in writing, you're set!" Nor can we say, "You can always tell if someone is lying over the phone!"

The rubber meets the road with that Dun & Bradstreet expression: "The deal isn't made until the money is paid."

Once that check is in hand (providing it's a good one), we might be able to relax, feeling that at least one part of the negotiation is over. That is, until we receive the next set of voicemails and emails that seem to point in opposite directions!

. . . .

Best Practice 16
Ask, "What Would Be Fair to You?"

In several experiments A was given $100 and instructed to share it with B in any manner he wished.

Often the $100 was split right down the middle. Sometimes A elected to keep more than $50 for himself. In the latter cases, when B was asked what he thought of the unequal distribution, repeatedly the word "unfair" came up. Though receiving any amount was a windfall to both A and B, there is a perception that if one party receives more, something is wrong.

Indeed there were occasions where B would say in effect, "To heck with this!" and stormed off in protest, spurning what he considered to be an unfair distribution.

Some negotiation pundits urge us *not* to close a gap in a proposed bargain by accepting an enticement to split the difference. They argue that if you split the difference more than once in the same deal, you've come out worse than if you had gradually edged your way back and forth to a mutually acceptable figure.

That may be true, but in the real world of business, I have never been asked to split the difference in rapid succession.

Even more significant is the fact that splitting the difference seems "fair," if only because both parties are agreeing to close a gap by conceding the exact same amount at the same time.

Americans especially are wedded to the concept of "fair dealing" between parties, and this exact phrase is seen in contract law, where "an implied covenant of good faith and fair dealing" is imputed to exist in every agreement.

For this reason, I suggest that on occasion—especially if you seem to be deadlocked and not making any progress—you float this question: "What would be fair to you?"

First, it signals that you're interested in achieving an equitable deal. Second, it gets the other party to make an offer, and if you accept, or even come close in your counteroffer, you'll probably strike a bargain that the other party will feel they can live with.

As I say so often in my seminar "Best Practices in Negotiation," there are exceptions to nearly every rule, including that one that urges us to avoid splitting the difference.

. . . .

Best Practice 17
Should You Grab Their First Offer?

Should you ever grab the first offer that your counterpart makes in a negotiation?

The answer is a firm "Never!" if you heed the advice given by a number of pundits.

The wisdom informing this is that if you gladly accept an initial offer, it sends the signal to your counterpart that you probably would have accepted less if he had ground you down a little.

Instead of being grateful that he made a fast deal, he'll always kick himself for not offering substantially less as his opening gambit.

As with so many rules of the game, this one has exceptions, as I note in my negotiation seminars.

1. If you're not dealing with a seasoned negotiator, the first offer he or she makes may be the best you'll hear. Practiced buyers will come in low and inch their way up based on give-and-take. But novices will typically throw out their best offer right away, leaving no room for haggling.

2. Your counterpart could be telling the truth when he says, "My budget for your speech is only $10,000 plus expenses." If you invest in trying to get him to budge from that figure, are you tacitly calling him a liar? Negotiation lore propagates the generalization that "buyers are liars," but this is obviously not applicable much of the time.

3. If there is a downside to seeming eager to do business with someone by accepting the first offer, there is an upside as well. You're saying just that: you're glad to earn their business. Enthusiasm has been called the highest-paid quality in the world, so how can it be the most costly one at the same time?

4. I can look back on some of the best deals I ever made, and many of them came after I simply said yes.

5. I can also look back on deals I've blown that would have made a big difference in my career had I said yes early in the negotiation. But I tried to be too clever, and I outsmarted myself.

When you go into a negotiation, you should know your latitudes of acceptance, rejection, and noncommitment. This means you should have a strong sense of what is a great or a good deal, a minimally acceptable one, and offers you will outright reject.

If the initial bid is in the first latitude, what's wrong with accepting? Yes, you might leave a few pennies on the table, but a speedy deal also delivers value, substantially cutting your transaction costs and the risk of alienating your counterpart with hardball tactics.

Judge each circumstance carefully, and when it comes to best practices, "Never say never!"

. . . .

Best Practice 18
Revive Dead Deals with Style!

Negotiations break off for several reasons:

1. Parties deadlock, digging into positions that settle like wet concrete.
2. Parties grow impatient, feeling the game isn't worth the effort.
3. Personalities offend.
4. External events, such as severe weather or stock market crashes, trump the proceedings.
5. Deadlines are reached, without results.

How can we revive deals once they seem to die? How do we get back on track?

One of the best starters is to let time pass. Give yourself and the other party some breathing room.

During the interval, both of you will very likely transition from feelings of indignation and self-righteousness to remorse: "Gee, it's too bad we couldn't work *something* out!" This is a positive mood to be in, because if there is at least a slight feeling of loss, you'll feel inclined to resume and to recoup.

Next, make the gesture of calling your counterparts, or better yet, if it's practical, try to bump into them or knock on their door.

Express gratitude for their time invested in the discussion, and mention that you feel bad you couldn't try a little harder to work something out.

Then stop talking and simply listen.

Typically, if there's even the faintest hint of a pulse in the deal, your counterpart will agree with you: it's too bad talks broke off.

At that moment, you are on the threshold of resuming your negotiations. It may take just one more statement or question to get up and running:

"Want to pick up where we left off?"

"Something occurred to me that I wanted to share with you. I think it makes a difference."

"I was a stickler on such-and-such a point, and I don't really think it's that important to me."

"I think I may have figured out how to give you what you need."

Take your pick, or mix and match these phrases. What's paramount is that you're interacting again, and communications are flowing.

Let time heal and provide you both with perspective, and after making the first move to break the silence, you're well on the way to bringing negotiations back to life.

Who knows? You both may benefit more than before because of the intermission.

. . . .

Best Practice 19
Detect the Three Types of Liars

One of the toughest decisions you'll make in negotiating is what to do once you have proof that your counterpart is a liar.

Do you cut off all contact, withdrawing on the spot from any current transactions? This isn't always possible, practical, or desirable, though, strictly speaking, you do have a justification to at least call for a pause in the action to determine whether you and your assets are at risk.

And is there a material difference between big lies—ones that misrepresent significant deal points—and little ones that seem irrelevant to the proceedings?

For instance, I was dealing with two executives at a franchise of a major services firm. One person revealed information to me about the other, not because I probed for it, but because they volunteered it. A few days later, one of them confessed that they were married to each other, though "for business purposes, we generally keep it a secret."

Their marital state was not relevant until it became clear they lied about it.

"Why lie?" I found myself wondering. Did it serve any purpose, except to alert me to the fact that they do lie, they practice deceit, and they're in the habit of using ruses? The disclosures each one made about the other's management practices didn't help.

Soon thereafter, I chose to sever our relationship, partly because I believe in the iceberg theory: if what you can see is treacherous, what lies below the surface is potentially devastating, so steer clear!

One of my law-school professors admonished those of us that were studying mediation with him: "99 percent of legal problems can be avoided if you simply deal with honest people."

But wasn't it the Greek philosopher Diogenes who wore out many sandals pounding the cobbles of ancient Athens, lamp in hand, seeking to find an honest man?

If we only do business with people who are completely honest, we might become very lonely negotiators.

I believe it is wise to make a few distinctions for practical purposes. There are three kinds of liars:

1. Those that do it where something major is at stake.
2. Those that lie about trivial things out of habit or seeking some thrill.
3. Those that exaggerate or negligently misrepresent facts without checking or supporting them with proof.

I would avoid dealing with the first two, Don't bother to accuse them of prevarication or mendacity. Just walk away, if you can't run. With the third, I'd proceed, but carefully, requesting documentation or substantiation for every assertion they make.

The adage, "Trust, but verify" is always good advice, especially when you're negotiating.

. . . .

Best Practice 20
Obvious Negotiation Tricks Fail

Some negotiators are a little too cute in how they play the game. They decide that a deal is an opportunity to assert their power, to preen, or to create confusion. They like being the center of attention, and while ostensibly striving for agreement, they're simply cruel kids pulling the wings off of bugs.

Their ploys, whether derived from purported negotiation gurus or hatched in the reptilian swamps of their own minds, will fail if they are obvious to their counterparts. Instead of creating consensus, obvious manipulators produce the opposite: distance and dissension.

When normal folks spot slithering snakes and gaping gators, we run the other way.

"Strategy" is a message that causes people to feel defensive. That "on guard" reflex—the suspicion that one is under attack or being taken advantage of—is *not* helpful to generating an agreement.

Above all, it provokes payback. When we're made to feel defensive, we tend to strike back with precisely the same tactic. Strategy begets strategy.

For example, there is a false truism in negotiation that I encountered first in the car business: "When there is a silence brought on by a deadlock in the conversation, he or she who speaks first loses."

The idea is that when pressure builds in both parties to say something, this leads one party to blurt out concessions, to cave in.

There's only one problem with this theory: *too many people know it!*

Consequently, both parties will be standing or sitting in front of each other, or worse, suspended in a phone conversation, expecting the other party to clear his throat first. It gets irritating, and after a certain point it simply seems rude. I believe this pushes the negotiation off a cliff.

If this sounds utterly childish and self-defeating, it is.

Speak up! Tell everyone you know, especially those that like to play their negotiations "cute," that tricks, gimmicks, and ploys are no substitute for good-faith communication.

. . . .

Best Practice 21
Urgency Works

Why this item? Why this price? Why buy from me? And above all, *why buy now?*

These are essential questions that all negotiators ask themselves.

The generic answer is that the item bargained for promises value, and value now is always more advantageous than value obtained later.

But really, if people think that value will be the same tomorrow as it is today, or worse, that the item will be cheaper—think iPhones and nearly every other piece of consumer technology—they'll have good reasons to wait.

If we want to produce positive cash flows today, this puts us in a deteriorating position. Is there a way to get people to believe that they are better advised to leap off the fence and onto our customer rolls?

Yes, it's called *urgency*, and it has probably been around since prehistoric days.

Cave Dweller 1: "Brrr! Winter is around the corner! Why don't you buy some pelts from me now so you won't freeze to death?"

Cave Dweller 2: "I think I'll wait to see what Glub is selling them for."

Cave Dweller 1: "Great idea, but I hear he just ran out of inventory, so I'm the only game in Stoneville. Lucky you, you're going to get my last dozen pelts, but only if you act right now, OK?"

Cave Dweller 2: "OK, but will you accept firewood in trade?"

Cave Dweller 1: "You're in luck."

Urgency takes a few forms, all of which are eminently familiar to us:
   • Limited supply.
   • The deadline is looming.
   • Prices are rising.

Urgency can come from without or within; it can be external or internal to the negotiations.

"The new car models are coming out, and they're going to cost 10 percent more than this year's."

"The price of gas is expected to climb by 20 percent by summer."

"They're discontinuing this toaster in bright yellow, so if this model works with your decor, buy now!"

"I'm retiring next week, and believe me, my replacement is one tough customer. Better cut a deal with me before he comes aboard."

"The federal tax credit expires on December 31."

"I have thirty minutes before I head to the airport. Either we put something together now, or we're out of luck."

Generally, it is easier to induce the other party to act now if the source of urgency seems to be something you don't personally control.

"The Chinese are experiencing the worst inflation they've had in decades, and they can't get enough skilled people into their factories. This is why we're expecting a whopping 35 percent cost increase. We're going to be forced to pass this on to you. But if you act now, you can get my current container price."

Why aren't appeals to urgency built into all negotiations? Because we get lucky: our counterparts, especially if they are unskilled, will create their own internal pressures to act now, thinking if they don't, they'll waste time, miss out, or simply be less than nice folks.

Of course, if you're the buyer, you want to play the other angle, saying, "There's no rush. I'd like to think about it."

Either way, use urgency to suit your objective, and remember to detect it when it's being used on you!

. . . .

Best Practice 22
Master the Clock

It's 9:00 on a Friday morning. I'm in the middle of a negotiation, and there is a pause in the action.

For strategic purposes, I have resolved that I will not communicate next. If this means the deal is off, so be it. I can and will live with that. But in the meantime, I'm carefully tracking the sequence of give-and-take, who is offering what, and, most importantly, *when*.

Clocking your negotiations is as critical to making a good deal as playing the clock is in football or basketball. Are my counterparts letting the clock run out, as I'm doing right now in this negotiation?

It's 9:15. If I get a call or an email pertaining to this deal within the next hour, this tells me something very important: my project is a high priority for my counterpart, because he has scheduled his contact during my prime time, my presumed first hour in the office. This would give me a chance to read and consider whatever he has to say and to come to terms before the weekend.

But if I don't hear from him until the afternoon, he's sending a signal that he wants me to ruminate over the deal points during Saturday and Sunday, and not to reflexively reject his offer.

If he waits until early next week to contact me, or if he doesn't respond for a full week or even two, he's still working the clock in a manner that's both visible and permissible to me.

Quietly, without fanfare, I'm charging him a "patience premium," a levy of a soon-to-be-determined amount that is predicated in part on his clockmanship. Sooner or later, without another round of communications, the clock will run out, and the game will be over.

As a seasoned negotiator, I realize this won't signify a win or a loss, but a draw, and this is a perfectly agreeable outcome.

. . . .

Best Practice 23
Try Fifteen Ways to Get That Discount

There are several ways to make any deal, yet for the most part, 99 percent of bargainers select the obvious path, which often leads to an impasse.

Business negotiators should practice their skills 24/7, especially when they have their consumer hats on. This enables them to try new tactics while matching wits with others they can learn from in a low-threat environment.

Let's say you want a stylish pair of shoes that is ridiculously overpriced. Passing by the store, you notice a hopeful sign: "Clearance!"

You scavenge for the pair that you like, and they're a perfect fit. But they aren't marked down. You ask to speak to the manager. He comes by with an imperious expression, and you wonder aloud why these aren't on sale.

"These never go on sale," he smirks with impatience, chastising you for even asking.

Here are fifteen ways to get that discount:

1. You can attack, claiming that his clearance sign is misleading advertising, fraudulently inducing passersby to come in. "Now, how much are you going to take off?"

2. You can smile back and ask: "Is this price the best you can do?"

3. You can make a specific offer of what you're willing to pay.

4. You can bake a bigger cake: "What if I purchase two pairs?"

5. You can start leaving the store. Some sellers will chase you down and reel you back in, especially if they have invested a lot of time with you (car dealers are famous for doing this).

6. You can make a ceremony out of writing down the make and model number of the shoe and say you'll shop for a better price, especially on the Internet.

7. You can ask: "Is the store closing? I can come back for the final sale."

8. "My friend Megan comes in all the time, and she gets discounts!"

9. "What other stores around here carry Bally?"

10. "Do you have an outlet store?"

11. "Can you sell them to me for your employee discount?"

12. "These are scratched. Are they seconds? They should be marked down!"

13. "I'll find them for less, but I'd rather find them here for less and give you the business. What can you do for me?"

14. "And what's the *cash* price?"

15. "If there's another markdown later, will you refund the difference?"

Typically, retailers look for a "keystone," which is two times the wholesale value they paid for inventory. So if the shoes retail for $240, this means the store may have invested $120, and perhaps even less. This leaves them a lot of wiggle room to discount and to still make a profit.

If you are a retailer, please note: there's no harm in rewarding your customers, especially if they're trying so hard to buy something from you. After all, isn't this why frequency marketing programs have been so successful in generating customer loyalty?

Practice bargaining 24/7, and you'll improve quickly.

. . . .

Best Practice 24
Take Donations in Lieu of Pay

When I was running an honors conference at a liberal-arts university, one of my guest lecturers, a chap I knew in grad school who had become a minor academic luminary, asked attendees at the end of his talk: "Would you pay me for the quality of information you received here?"

He wasn't asking them for money, but to endorse the value of what he had already tendered.

Finding his question quirky, counterintuitive, and an odd way to negotiate support, I chatted with him later on and impishly admonished: "The key, my friend, isn't whether an audience will pay to get out; it's whether they'll pay to get in!"

I went on to have a very successful career in consulting, and even wrote a how-to book on the topic, partly to straighten out knowledgeable but commercially confused colleagues such as my pal, who simply didn't have the best financial instincts.

However, times have changed.

As I've noted in many articles, the Internet has ushered in an age in which lots and lots of folks refuse to pay anything up front to get into seminars or to access information products such as consulting and articles. Search engines like Google have spoiled them, giving the impression that there are hundreds if not more authorities on every topic, and that some will advise without charge.

Given the ubiquity of "free," I think we might want to reconsider our salary negotiation strategy. We can start by revisiting my academic buddy's concept of paying to get out, though the tale I'm about to tell will put a different spin on it.

I visited a life coach upon the urging of my relatives, who expressed bona fide satisfaction with the results he produced in their lives.

This gentleman did not charge by the hour or consultation, which in my case lasted about ninety minutes, including an introductory "Why I'm here and what I hope to get" recital.

That is, he didn't negotiate a given rate, but said, quite affably, that he did accept donations. Some of the oil paintings in his Western-style living room, for instance, were gifts for services.

I elected to simply hand him some cash.

He seemed pleased, and I was in the same mood, because his ministrations were calming, and I wanted to express gratitude for helping those I love to feel a little happier.

Giving him a reward also made me feel benevolent, whereas paying him a specific preordained amount might have made me feel reluctant or remorseful, or may have agitated the miser in me.

Odd how voluntarism works!

Anyway, I'm going to try it. The next few times I am asked for my expert opinion, I'll state that there is no charge, but I do accept donations.

I'm especially interested in discovering: (1) whether ardent nonpayers will begin to pay; and (2) whether those that are used to paying will pay less, the same, or more.

. . . .

Best Practice 25
Every Deal Must Stand on Its Own

When I was twenty-one, I brought a deal to the president of our leasing company for his approval.

He looked it over, and with a stern face asked me a few quick, penetrating questions.

"How much is this car costing us? What markup are you using? And why is our margin so slim?"

I replied that I knew the deal was thin, but I was trying to win a fleet deal from the CEO of a major public company. I thought that if I did well for him on the first car, I might get a contract for a hundred more.

Slowly, my boss navigated his reading specs to the end of his nose, striking a stern, fatherly pose like Benjamin Franklin.

"Gary, there's no such thing as losing money on the first deal and then making it up in volume."

To which he added in a louder voice, building to a crescendo: "Every deal must stand on its own!"

Fortune smiled upon me in a roundabout way. When I delivered the car, the executive rejected it, because he disliked the color of the interior leather. This forced me to find a substitute, which actually cost my firm less money, making what had been the skinniest of deals somewhat plumper.

But the lesson didn't escape me. Profit enables us to stay in business today and remain in business tomorrow. The larger our profit, the better equipped we are to serve our clientele in both the short and long run.

Profit is not an unearned premium, as buyers would like to make us believe. Nor is it a windfall. It is a necessary ingredient of doing business.

Whenever someone grinds down your initial price, hinting, "There's more where this came from!" be suspicious. Usually it's a ploy, and often it's a lie. They don't plan to buy anything except the discounted morsel you provided.

Moreover, as my boss noted, there's no such thing as losing money on the first unit and then making it up in volume. That approach to negotiating will doom your company.

Don't be bashful. Tell prospects who are relentlessly shopping price while promising the moon that every deal must stand on its own.

. . . .

Best Practice 26
Offer Guarantees (and Get Them Too)

In tough times, most negotiators look for a rock-solid closer, a line or an inducement that will put deals over the top and nudge fence-sitters and naysayers into accepting the terms put forth.

In my experience, there are few devices that are as useful in this respect as the guarantee. At its most generous, it tells your counterpart that if they're not happy, the deal can be undone. It takes the risk out of saying yes, and it has a special status in the law, where it is called a contract "subject to a condition subsequent."

Certain businesses were built on the guarantee. I worked for one of them, Time-Life Books, cutting my teeth in sales and sales management. We sold our wares on the famous ten-day trial basis. Buyers had ten days with any and all of our titles. If they were displeased, they could return them without further obligation. This closer moved millions of books into households whose members never stepped into bookstores.

Were some of these books returned? Of course, but we learned enough to know that the products themselves were not wholly responsible for that outcome.

How we sold, the exact words we used, and the placement of the guarantee in our message accounted for whether an extra 25 percent of trial takers would become book collectors or not.

It boiled down to whether we *oversold the guarantee*. If we put too much emphasis on it, in effect "training" our prospects to perceive their "out" or deal breaker as a desirable or equally agreeable outcome, they'd follow our lead and send books back.

On the other hand, if we mentioned the guarantee prominently but then assured listeners that they would want to retain the volumes, negotiating with them to make a fair appraisal, that's what they'd do, in numbers that were statistically significant.

So if you're seeking a dealmaker, especially in tough times, negotiating a guarantee might do the trick, providing you don't push it too hard. But once you have decided to adopt this contingency, you need to organize your entire business around it. After that point, it will have cascading effects well beyond sales, affecting customer service, credit and collections, and especially cash flow and receivables management.

But accepted wisdom says the guarantee is so powerful that when properly drafted and presented, it is well worth the adjustments it ushers in.

. . . .

Best Practice 27
Read Your Counterpart's Pain Threshold

I was reading an archived *New York Times* article from April 21, 1999, written by former Defense Secretary Robert S. McNamara, a primary architect of our strategy in the Vietnam War.

He invested much of his postgovernment career in contrition for what he had come to believe was a misguided war. One of his constructive actions was to seek out expert feedback here and in postwar Vietnam to determine how strategy on both sides could have gone so wrong.

These exchanges revealed to McNamara that during the war "each side miscalculated by repeatedly underestimating the costs and risks its adversary was willing to accept." North Vietnam was "prepared to absorb far greater punishment than was ever delivered by the American bombing."

At the same time, McNamara realized, the "Hanoi Government, in a series of disastrous miscalculations made from 1961 to 1965, repeatedly underestimated America's willingness to prosecute the war in the South on the ground, and in the North via the bombing."

Preoccupied with inflicting as much pain as possible, the parties apparently never seriously considered the idea of installing a "neutral coalition government" in South Vietnam, which, however enduring, might have been mutually agreeable.

For students of negotiation, the first question that comes to mind is how can we accurately assess our counterpart's inclination to bear pain, to persist in a state of siege or relative privation?

If we're using the stick instead of a carrot, seeking leverage through aversive means, is there a way of determining how much pain is necessary to do the job?

Most significantly, are there certain adversaries that will fight to the death, permitting complete destruction of their assets or culture, to deny an adversary an enduring advantage or victory?

Lest you think that these big-picture questions don't apply to everyday negotiations, consider how often people storm away from the bargaining table over apparent trifles. Not only do they shut down the process, often they vow to inflict pain on their counterparts through expensive, protracted legal proceedings.

Couples who terminate their marriages in acrimony wage wars that scar the emotional landscape, stripping both parties of the financial assets they'll need to rebuild their lives.

In such conflicts, there is often the perception that one party can prevail through sheer grit, toughness, or belligerency, expressed in a willingness to outspend or simply out-endure the other.

But it is clear to nearly any uninvolved spectator how needlessly brutal and mutually defeating such conflicts are. In fact, victory is to be gained only by sparing each other as much misery as possible and by seeking détente as quickly as possible.

Perhaps the best method of assessing a counterpart's pain threshold is to avoid calculating it with the illusion of statistical refinement (one of McNamara's tendencies).

Instead, assume your counterpart's ability to persist while hurting is so substantial that by using the stick, even the biggest and most brutal, you won't prevail. Or if you do, there will be so much collateral damage and reconstruction to be done after the fighting has stopped that the cleanup and healing will never eradicate your stains and scars.

Without the stick, what tools are we left with?

A chastened McNamara might say, "Diplomacy."

. . . .

Best Practice 28
Recognize the Five Ways Car Dealers Beat You

At the end of a recent holiday weekend, I hastily left a car dealership with a relative in tow.

If we hadn't bolted, she would have succumbed to that heady combination of new car smells wafting through the dealership and the superior negotiation skills of the sales staff.

Car dealers have been sharpening their negotiating talons for more than a century, so they have a bag of tricks that can hypnotize almost all shoppers, no matter how savvy they might be in other contexts.

Specifically, there are five ways dealers get the drop on customers in negotiations:

1. Dealers know how to negotiate. They practice negotiating every day, and practice makes them sharper in nearly every way. They are used to putting on their game faces, cozying up to shoppers, gabbing about inessentials to create trust, and getting folks to express an urgent desire to buy TODAY! Most folks only shop for cars every three or four years, at a minimum. Who is going to be in the groove, a person that is in a Super Bowl every day or someone that has been warming the bench each of the last 1,500 days?

2. Dealers know what their costs are, and you don't. This is an essential baseline in negotiations. For all of the presumed transparency ushered in by the web regarding "dealer costs" and "dealer invoice," these figures are still inflated. Manufacturers offer secret incentives and rebates that are known only to dealers, and civilians simply don't have access to them.

3. Dealers know the market for both new cars and used cars. This gives them a big edge in negotiating to buy your old car, or declining to buy it, and in holding firm or being flexible on hot or cold new inventory.

4. Dealers know one another. They understand that their competitors cannot and will not cut their own throats, doing anything and everything in negotiations to make deals. So, within ranges, there is tacit price fixing. You just won't get local dealers especially to break ranks. Out-of-state or out-of-town dealers might have more incentive to bargain at lower prices.

5. Dealers know you. Sure, officially you're strangers: you've never met. But by asking you a few quick

questions and by observing your body language and the car you drove in, they can surmise whom they're negotiating with and how urgently you want to acquire a new ride.

So appreciate from the get-go that dealers will use these advantages to eke out a nifty profit while bleating that you are bleeding them dry.

Do your homework before you negotiate with dealers. Be prepared to work one dealer against the next. Whatever you do, don't feel sorry for them. It's just another way they get the drop on you in negotiations.

. . . .

Best Practice 29
Bring in a New Face

"Megan is going to be joining us today!" I beamed to my negotiation counterpart, who instantly appeared nervous and off-balance.

"She wasn't available yesterday," I explained. "Where did we leave off?"

Suddenly Robert needed to recite our progress to date, feeling that he needed to obtain Megan's endorsement on every point. This put him in a one-down position.

I didn't bring Megan in because she is a crackerjack negotiator. I recruited her because two on one almost always confers an advantage to the team.

Moreover, when the teammate is a surprise addition, it tends to put all that was "accomplished" beforehand into suspension, pending her approval. If any concessions were made (in this case because Robert was quick-witted or extra charming or persuasive), it could be corrected in Megan's presence.

Robert said, "We had agreed to do X."

"Let's revisit that point, Robert, because I wanted to air that out a little more."

All of a sudden, everything that seemed to be set in stone, at least in Robert's mind, was in sand, and the winds were reshaping it.

A confederate doesn't have to actively participate; generally, it is more productive if he or she doesn't, opting instead to observe and report to you during breaks. This way she can detect "tells," nonverbal giveaways that indicate how your counterpart truly feels about a given matter.

A variant of bringing in a fresh face is substituting for a negotiator or being suddenly substituted for. This is especially valuable if the first negotiator isn't pleased with the results he has achieved to date.

The simple act of substituting makes the other side of the negotiations labor extra hard to reestablish rapport, and to wonder if everything that seemed to be a done deal would unravel.

If you are on the other side of this gambit, it can certainly seem like a dirty trick. But don't panic. You can always reschedule for a time when the first negotiator will be able to resume.

In any case, check to see if the substitute has sufficient authority to make a deal today without running the agreement by the first bargainer or anyone else.

If he says he can't seal a deal, that's all the more reason to wait for someone across the table who can.

· · · · · · · · · · · · · ·

Best Practice 30
Cool Down Overheated Negotiations with Transition Phrases

Why do so many negotiations stalemate? Why do parties dig into entrenched positions and refuse to budge?

There are left-brained and right-brained answers to this perplexity.

The left brain is reputed to be rational, so let's look to logic and to the observable data of negotiations. According to Harvard research (about the most left-brained source we can find), parties stalemate because they use positional negotiating. They set certain deal points, often denominated in money terms, and they relentlessly stick to them.

"I must get at least $16,000 for this car!"

"But I can only pay $15,000," replies the buyer.

Instantly—and this term is important—the seller repeats his position.

"Sorry, the price is $16,000."

Just as quickly, the respondent says, "No can do."

With those rapid-fire replies, the deal is off. Typically, participants don't like each other enough to try again.

The right-brained explanation is that we become emotional. Our ego gets involved in getting our way, of which our stated price is the symbol.

"I want it!"

"You can't have it!"

Same outcome, unless we buy precious moments to cool things down so we can explore the other person's rationale for offers and counteroffers and quiet our raging feelings.

I suggest you use transition phrases such as:

Well, I understand that, but . . .

Well, I appreciate that, but . . .

Well, I respect that, but . . .

You will sound agreeable without agreeing to the terms of the deal. You'll also give yourself about three to five seconds to revise your strategy.

For example, research suggests that you might try this gambit:

"Well, I respect that, but how did you arrive at that specific figure?" Here you're seeking to understand the rationale leading the person to select his position.

"I have to pay off my bank loan of $15,250, so I can't accept $15,000."

Now the buyer knows how much bargaining room is in the deal. He can agree to pay off the loan, coming up in his offer by $250, or he can sweeten the deal even more.

Slowing down the clock is crucial to becoming composed enough to keep the transaction alive.

Transition phrases can help.

. . . .

Best Practice 31
Why No Strategy Is the Worst Strategy

I have trained countless salespeople who believe they are naturals, that anything they do is bound to achieve great results and put business on the books.

Their self-confidence is admirable, and I suppose that it, along with a certain amount of bluster, does see them through to a given number of orders.

But there are few naturals in negotiating.

While in selling, being nice and agreeable might induce certain prospects to spontaneously buy, the same traits in a negotiation are a prescription for conceding too much while emboldening our counterparts to exact uneven advantages.

There are five reasons that no strategy is the worst strategy in negotiations:

1. Walking into a negotiation with no strategy is like going into battle without ammunition. It's a prescription for disaster. If you haven't carefully laid out your objective, you're very unlikely to secure it.

2. You might want to appear spontaneous, because this can relax or disarm your counterpart. But actually being spontaneous will induce you to overtalk and overcommit. Loose lips sink ships, right?

3. You'll forget essential bargaining points unless you outline them carefully. Once bargaining has officially concluded, it will be difficult to restart it smoothly.

4. You'll be lured into traps and step on land mines if there is no safe path that you have preplowed.
5. You'll fail to research your opponent, and his or her probable goals, tactics, and constraints. Without intelligence, you'll be negotiating against yourself.

If you bargain for a living, as many attorneys and purchasing professionals do, you will win and lose with a frequency that will be humbling. You'll tend to take very little for granted. Above all, you'll prepare quite carefully. You might even delay or bow out of proceedings for which you haven't had sufficient time to strategize.

. . . .

Best Practice 32
Make Your Counterpart See the Value You See

I was selling a piece of prime real estate, and more than one realtor thought my price was too high, pointing to the comps for our area.

Comps comes from the word *comparable*. The fundamental idea is that similar properties should be priced and sold for similar amounts of money.

So far, so good. I have no argument with that precept. But I take issue with the metric that is widely used to establish similarity.

In residential real estate, it has primarily been square footage. If the average price of homes sold in an area has been $250,000, and the average size has been 2,500 square feet, this means that houses in the area are fetching $100 per square foot.

Bringing a 2,500-square-foot home onto the market at $250,000 is a safe bet. You might be able to stretch that to $275,000 if it is upgraded, with a relatively new kitchen. But once you pass $280,000, you're going to meet resistance.

The implicit agreement among realtors, home buyers, lenders, and nearly everyone else is that folks are buying and selling square footage, but they are not.

Every piece of real estate is unique. Some places are custom-built or designed especially for their lots by respected architects, making them more beautiful than others. The home I was selling fit into this category.

It was one of a kind, quite unique, a midcentury glass-and-beam gem. By no means was it anything close to that fictional "average." It wasn't a box. It curved with the landscape and was snugly part of it.

For this reason, I'd paid more than the comp price, and I expected more upon its sale.

In real estate, there are several ways to arrive at a commercial property's value. Replacement cost is one of them, taking labor, materials, and land value into account.

Location and area foot traffic might be the most important factors in pricing a property for a fast-food location.

Market value—what a willing seller and a willing buyer would agree to—is another method.

Every now and then, a person or a business will come along with a nonconforming use in mind, making a spot worth disproportionately more. For instance, an industrial area with factories might be wanted for a dance club or to redevelop into artists' lofts.

Know this: property values, like nearly all values, are always subject to dispute and to differing calculation by the parties.

You should never accept a price as set in stone, or as being "scientifically" or authoritatively derived. At the basis of most pricing is a guess, a hope, a rough estimate, a reference to past values, or outright arbitrariness.

We can see this comes in the retail sector, where prices are printed on items. Car stickers contain references to MSRP—manufacturer's suggested retail pricing. It sounds credible and impressive, especially because MSRP is repeated in advertising, so we're used to hearing it as an anchor.

But this is simply the manufacturer saying, "I think the retailer might reasonably charge and get this amount for the gizmo I've made." It's in the manufacturer's interest to set the MSRP as high as possible, giving it the ability to charge the highest possible prices and enabling the retailer to follow suit.

But it's an arbitrary price.

During graduate school, I sold Bic ballpoint pens by the gross to restaurants. The model I sold, the PF-49, bore a price of 49 cents. It was imprinted onto the barrel of each pen.

My boss "sold" them to me at 16 cents, and I resold them to eateries at 33 cents, more than any other salesperson attempted to get. What were they worth? What was their value?

I suppose up to the 49-cent mark that appeared on the barrel. If that had been covered up or painted over, who knows what the pen could have sold for? $1.49?

When someone says, "I'm selling you this *at cost*," what does this mean, and what factors are being used to arrive at that cost?

Book publishers historically have sold (actually consigned) their publications to bookstores for 60 percent of the retail price. What if the titles don't sell quickly?

They might be remaindered, which means repriced to outlets at 10 or 20 percent of retail value. They find their way to the bargain tables at the same bookstores, where they are put on sale at 50 percent off retail price. Everybody is still coming out pretty well, even though it seems that the books are being moved at distressed prices.

In one case we discuss and role-play in my Best Practices in Negotiation course, there is an ideal buyer for a piece of mixed-use real estate. The essential question isn't what is the property worth. It is:

What is the property worth to HIM?

He is a "market of one," an absolutely unique negotiation partner. Theoretically, because of his training, experience, savvy, credentials, and physical location, he could buy the property for disproportionately more money than a similar person situated in the same town.

Ultimately, this is the key question we must address with everyone:

What is their perceived value of the item being bargained for? Can I influence this perception in a manner that favors me and creates a better negotiated outcome?

Sometimes negotiating with certain folks is like trying to teach a bear to sing. You won't succeed, and you'll only annoy the bear and upset yourself. They simply won't perceive the value that you believe you are tendering.

You can't persuade all of the people all of the time, but that still means some folks will understand and respond to your value proposition.

Keep seeking them out.

. . . .

Best Practice 33
Don't Be Impulsive

I accompanied a relative to a car dealership yesterday after having briefed her thoroughly on our purchasing strategy.

Correction: It was more of a nonpurchasing strategy, because one of the fundamental planks of our negotiation platform was this agreement: "No matter what, you are *not* going to drive out of the lot with a car—not today, right?"

The idea of not buying during the first visit involves psychology on both sides of the bargaining table.

1. It is a prophylaxis against our tendency to get too excited and immediately buy something other than the best vehicle at less than favorable terms.

2. It proves to the dealer that we're serious about getting the best possible deal, and we have the willpower and smarts to walk away and hit the reset button. This means he is going to compete for the business if he wants to get it.

"No problem," my comrade-in-arms concurred. This visit was exploratory, preliminary, and for show.

All of that got thrown out the window.

She was steered to a car that she test-drove and which seemed suitable. It was an upgrade from her last ride, which had been totaled in a crash precipitated by a red-light runner.

The salesperson started high, saying the car was worth $18,500, but she'd give it away at $16,000, making only a $200 profit. To her credit, my colleague said she'd think it over, but it was clear to the seller that buying mania had started to take over. This is the voice inside that says: "I have found *exactly* what I want, and I *must* have it now, and she says it's a really good deal, so nothing is going to stop me!"

Slow down . . . please!

1. There are millions of unsold cars in the United States right now. It only stands to reason that hundreds if not many thousands of them would be just as "perfect."

2. You want it now, because it is a change, a reward, and it represents an end to this very uncomfortable process of acquiring a new set of wheels.

3. Nothing says you must have this car except you. Somehow you have made it to this moment in your life without this transporter, and you can make it another few days or a week, which is what it will take to get a better deal.

4. Of course the dealer is going to say it is a good deal! They are masters at putting numbers in front of people while seeming to dramatically discount them.

5. The fear of missing out is propelling you, and if you can't put the brakes on your own impulsiveness, you are out of control. You'll sign anything on any terms to get what you have now rationalized you deserve.

I intervened.

Like an expert car appraiser, I checked out the windshield of the car. There were pits in the line of vision, indicating the windshield should be replaced. The dealer cost is $150–$200.

The paint was pitted on the leading edge of the hood, but instead of repainting the entire hood, the dealer touched up the surface, leaving perceptible bumps and dots. The dealer cost to repaint a metallic finish is $200–$300.

And I had just begun. The seller said she'd have to talk to her manager, and he skated over in a flash, just as quickly hitting the wall. No, he wouldn't replace or credit the value of the windshield.

Anyway, this was a great deal!

Wrong again. It was a full-pop retail deal, I told him, as a "special sales" red card revealed that was tucked into the front seat.

If your heart is racing, and you're in love, you won't stop to see these demerits. In fact, your eyes will glaze over and you'll be stuck in la-la land.

Always take a break from the action when you're buying a car.

Your battle isn't you against them.

It's you against that ravenous, impulsive consumer that is in the mirror—if you dare to look.

. . . .

Best Practice 34
Use the Ten Deal Points That Don't Pertain to Price

Bill, everybody's favorite salesman, has fallen into a slump. When you ask him what's wrong, he says: "It's price, price, price. Everybody wants a better deal."

As long as Bill treats price as an objection, he'll keep selling value, which is what modern doctrine urges. And the glaze will come over his prospects' eyes, and he'll miss closing another deal.

What's wrong with selling value, with saying that you get what you pay for and your product is worth the investment? You're still talking about *money*. And as long as it is about money, as with the proverbial sword, you'll live and die by it. You need to change the buyer's base of thinking, getting him off price. How do you do that?

You NEGOTIATE.

But isn't negotiation about money, money, money? Yes and no.

Price is just one aspect of any deal. Let's look at a true commodity business, such as copper wire.

In theory, copper is copper, right? It's a basic element on the periodic table. And if it's rolled into wire, well, wire is wire, with only so many gauges.

If it's a commodity, and you can get it nearly anywhere, what is there to differentiate one supplier from the next? It all boils down to price, so the company with the cheapest price should get 100 percent of the market, correct? But it doesn't, and it never has.

Why? Price is just one element of competitive advantage. People are influenced by lots of other things.

Among them you'll find: (1) habit; (2) convenience; (3) personalized attention; (4) credibility; (5) trust; (6) reliability; (7) customer service; (8) power; (9) friendship; and (10) loyalty.

I've just listed ten important dimensions of deals that Bill is ignoring, needlessly extending that slump of his. And each of these factors can be negotiated. Price is significant, but by far it isn't the only factor in buying decisions.

Tap into the others, and price will be just one more dimension of a deal, an invitation to negotiate and not a show-stopping objection.

· · · · · · · · · · · · · ·

Best Practice 35
Seize Everyday Negotiating Opportunities

In my negotiation seminar, I invest much of my time teaching big-ticket bargaining. This is only natural, because we intuitively believe we have the most at stake when we're negotiating for cars, homes, better compensation, and on behalf of our employers.

But if you take a closer look at the sheer number of opportunities we have to negotiate, most of them involve transactions that fly under the radar—small exchanges at supermarkets and local retailers.

For example, today I tendered two coupons for baby food. These are valuable, offering one dollar off each. But there's a catch, as I found out yesterday when I handed them to an overly scrutinizing clerk.

I had to buy specific quantities not only of that brand, but of certain subbrands, such as organic this or that, or vitamin-fortified foods.

Talk about picky! Well, I said to him, "No problem. Let's just eliminate the baby food from my order, and I'll come back on another day and get the right items."

He was a little surprised. I didn't buckle under to the retail prices, and I wasn't afraid of losing face by implicitly saying, "Look. Without coupons, these foods aren't worth the money!"

Today I came back with a different strategy.

1. I resolved to forum-shop, which in the law means selecting the court or judge who is most sympathetic to your cause. In the supermarket, this means standing in the line of a "nice" clerk.
2. I decided I'd comply with one of two of the manufacturer's requirements. I would buy the right number of items, but I would only buy what we use—the main brands and not the exotic subbrands.
3. I tendered the coupons after all of my items were scanned instead of handing them to the clerk first. In my experience, clerks are less meticulous in lawyering the fine print if they receive the coupons after the whole order is rung up.

It worked, and the clerk remarked, "Hey, those are great coupons!"

No kidding.

If you want to refine your negotiation skills, use your common sense to

1. Forum-shop, selecting the best negotiation counterpart;
2. Use partial compliance with the apparent deal requirements, but sticking to your ultimate preferences on the major points; and
3. Be sensitive to the order in which you introduce deal points, noting that when the horses have left the gate, it's easier for someone to go with the stampede instead of declaring a false start.

One more thing: Don't wait for big-ticket occasions to polish your bargaining skills. Burnish them every day, in every way!

· · · · · · · · · · · · · · ·

Best Practice 36
Don't Give Too Much or Get Too Little

There is a clear point I make in my "Best Practices in Negotiation" seminars:

The more you ask for, the more you'll get!

Another point is:

Don't be afraid to tender a fractional offer!

The problem with sellers and buyers who take these tips to heart in the same transaction is that they'll probably stalemate. The seller will seem greedy, and the buyer will seem to be trying to get a "steal."

How can you know when you've crossed the line from reasonable to unreasonable demand in setting a selling or buying price?

You can't know with utter certitude. But you can map out fairly reliable latitudes of acceptance, rejection, and noncommitment.

These are zones of acceptability and unacceptability.

For example, let's say you are trying to buy a piece of real estate in a relatively stable market. Obviously, the asking or listing price is *acceptable* to the seller. Anything below the sum total of the loans against the property, plus commissions and other fees and taxes, will be *unacceptable*. (Note: I'm not talking about short sales that can be made in distorted and depressed real estate markets.)

Between the acceptable and unacceptable zones is a zone of *noncommitment*, one of latitude, where there's haggling room.

If you offer in the noncommitment zone, you'll probably evoke a counteroffer, and the negotiation game will continue, perhaps to a mutually agreeable conclusion. But if you start with an offer in the rejection zone, you risk offending the seller, who might reject you and your offer, vowing not to give you another bite at the apple.

If you set a price that is far beyond anything comparable on the market, buyers will think you're crazy or unrealistic. In other words, you'll be priced in the rejection zone, and you simply won't see any offers.

The adages "Start high and you can always cut your price" and "Start low and you can always come up" don't work that well when pushed to extremes in the real world of negotiations.

So what do we do? Start high or low, depending on whether you are the seller or buyer, but do so within a proper range of tolerance, remaining within the latitudes of acceptance and noncommitment.

. . . .

Best Practice 37
Play the Scarcity Card and Win

As you've read in these pages, I spent some time in the car business. When we think of that industry, we tend to envision new-car dealerships, replete with rows of gleaming, just-manufactured vehicles.

This image comes to mind partly because much of the expensive advertising on TV, radio, and other media comes from new-car promotions. But a lot of business-people prefer entering the used-car part of the field.

Their reasoning? Every car on the lot is unique, one of a kind, making it a lot easier to tout than a model that is plentiful and available in nearly every town in the country.

For instance, while Detroit might have made thousands of 1966 Ford Mustang convertibles, there is only this one, in yellow, in this specific body condition, with this precise equipment and mileage on the odometer, that is here on my lot.

Grab it before someone else does!

This is a credible inducement to buy now, on my terms. You simply cannot effectively comparison-shop a used car. Sure, certain ballpark values can be assigned to any vehicle, even from afar through Internet research, yet who knows when a similar, let alone identical, car will come onto the market?

I know a successful businessman who sells industrial tools. He plays the scarcity card like a shark. First, he'll do a broadcast fax to tout some device. In that document, he'll put a inventory "meter" in a box at the top.

"ONLY 5,250 REMAINING. THESE WILL SELL OUT BY NEXT WEEK. BUY NOW!"

He'll call his list a few days later, on Tuesday, and tell them, after touting the benefits of the item, "We're down to only 2,200 left in inventory. I'll hold just 600 pieces for you for 48 hours, but I need your purchase order then, OK?"

On Wednesday, another fax will go out, indicating only 980 are left.

On Thursday morning, he'll call the prospects back. "I'm holding your 600 pieces, but I can sell them to somebody else. Do you want them?"

There are two sources of motivation, especially for businesspeople: (1) the desire for gain and (2) the fear of loss.

Scarcity, the way the tool honcho above uses it, taps into the fear of loss.

It's always amazing to see how many otherwise calm and deliberate buyers are put into a frenzy by the possibility of losing an opportunity.

How do you counter a scarcity ploy?

You can argue the opposite: that this car isn't the only Mustang convertible for sale in the area, nor is it the best example of one, or at the most attractive price.

Plus, your heart isn't all that set on getting a Mustang. You're flexible, looking at Camaros, Cougars, and Firebirds of that vintage too.

If you're the buyer, you say that an item is common, widely available, interchangeable, and with no special characteristics.

If you're the seller, you argue for the item's scarcity and unique qualities.

By the way, the same arguments pertain to selling services. Dr. Knowitall might contend, "I am the best board-certified ophthalmologist in the area, with over 50,000 surgeries personally performed."

"Hey, LASIK is a widely known technique," you could reply. "And in our metropolitan area I can choose from more than fifty experienced establishments that perform the same surgery. The only difference is price. Are you going to offer a more attractive fee than Dr. Justasgood?"

Play the scarcity card either way and win!

. . . .

Best Practice 38
Counter Dirty Tricks

I've been negotiating contracts as an entrepreneur and lawyer for more than twenty years, and I've found that one of the greatest challenges in making deals is countering the dirty tricks others try to pull on us.

Dirty tricks range from purposely missing deadlines to poor-mouthing—contending you have little or no money—to outright lying about pertinent details, such as the individual's power to approve deals on their own.

What countermeasures can we deploy without using deceptive and underhanded tactics ourselves?

One of the best ways to chasten a scurrilous counterpart is to call them on their tactics, to bring them out into the open instead of reflexively reacting.

For instance, I was negotiating the deal points of a proposed training program with the VP of sales at a large manufacturing company in the heart of the Midwest. He seemed less than completely aboveboard (to state it nicely), casting darting glances here and there, consulting little note cards as we chatted.

So I asked him: "Whose techniques are you using in this negotiation: Nierenberg, Cohen, or Karrass?" These are the names of some widely known experts.

He cleared his throat and replied, sheepishly, "Karrass."

"Ah," I sighed and nodded, smiling all the while.

That little challenge brought him back into the here and now, and he seemed much less strategic and more spontaneous, enabling us to quickly forge a suitable agreement.

If you can actually name the ploy someone is using, that's even better. If two negotiators are on the same team and one is especially nice while the other is obnoxious, you can remark:

"Hey, you two are using 'good cop, bad cop,' aren't you?"

Educate yourself in what to expect by studying the best practices in negotiation. Forewarned is forearmed.

. . . .

Best Practice 39
No Job Offer? Negotiate Reconsideration!

First, Derek was shocked, then flummoxed, then outraged, and finally energized.

An email stated that his application had been rejected for a teaching position because he "failed to meet minimum qualifications" for the post.

That was a hoot. His credentials so surpassed the minimal requirements that they probably put to shame 99 percent of the other applicants.

Clearly something was wrong, and Derek suspected cronyism and bias. He knew it was up to him to negotiate a reconsideration of his application.

He called the human-resources department and spoke to one of the application's processors. She scanned his credentials, saw they were many and sufficient, and couldn't come up with a rationale that would support his rejection.

A day or two later, Derek got a voice mail from the processor, saying his application was rejected because it was not completely filled out and in one spot he merged two pieces of information.

That lame excuse wasn't going to wash either. Before the application deadline, he had been informed by another clerk that his file was complete.

He phoned up the chain of command, stating specifically that there were "irregularities" and "inconsistent and inadequate stories" being told on different days to explain his rejection.

He stated, calmly and clearly, that he was willing to pursue legal action to right this wrong.

A few days elapsed, and he received an email indicating his application would be considered with the others after all, and he'd be informed if an interview would be offered.

In light of his vigorous and contentious pursuit, what are his chances of (1) being extended an interview and (2) receiving serious and fair consideration for the position?

They aren't good, but he still has a shot at employment because he wouldn't take an uninformed, erroneous, or underhanded rejection as final. Because he hung in there, he is a winner.

If you believe that you are the victim of bias or cronyism, or that your applications are not being given fair consideration, bring it to the attention of the hiring authorities.

Escalate matters until you reach senior people who will investigate on your behalf. If after you have exhausted your administrative remedies, you are still not satisfied, seek legal counsel.

You may be entitled to money damages or to an actual job offer.

. . . .

Best Practice 40
Negotiate Less Job Stress

I've just finished writing an article advising people to beware of the collateral damage that certain career choices can incur.

From personal experience and observation, I pointed out that two occupations I am familiar with—practicing law and selling automobiles—can be hazardous to one's health.

These careers are pressure cookers: they can elevate blood pressure, contribute to nervous conditions, and even spawn addictions.

In my negotiation course, we discuss job-related negotiations, covering salaries, benefits, job assignments, occupational objectives, and job evaluation criteria.

In one case, called "Bud and Shirley," we get into the thorny issue of workplace stress. We focus on an employee who has been informally tasked with mentoring and coaching new employees, though he doesn't have a supervisor's or a trainer's title or pay scale. He's stressed to the max, suggesting that a fight-or-flight reaction is imminent.

This is not a good circumstance for anyone, or for the company, yet scenarios like it are commonplace. People are pushed to the breaking point, but they are reluctant to volunteer information about their plight lest they be seen as slackers or expendable troublemakers.

Still, something has to give, to ease the pressure and prevent an explosion.

The good news is workplace stress can be negotiated. The pace of our labors, the cooperation we get from others, and the general mood of the environment can be discussed and, by agreement, be improved.

Know that effective negotiation goes well beyond the subject of money. It affects nearly everything, including things that are worth much more.

. . . .

Best Practice 41
Never Negotiate against Yourself

The Los Angeles Dodgers and agent Scott Boras were at an impasse. They were negotiating Manny Ramirez's 2009 contract. The team offered a two-year deal, while Manny's agent asserted it would take four years or more to tango.

Dodgers general manager Ned Colletti tried to avoid what is called *negotiating against oneself*.

If you're the only or top bidder for something, the traditional negotiating playbook says:

1. Wait for a counteroffer before sweetening your original offer.

2. If you receive silence instead of a counteroffer in return, the other party will blink. If he has received no better offer than yours from a third party, he'll have to deal with you sooner or later and accept yours.

3. If you succumb to your impatience or buckle under pressure from the approach of a deadline (such as the start of spring training) and offer a better deal before receiving a counteroffer, you'll make concessions for nothing.

In that case, you are bidding against yourself and throwing away money.

Boras knew all this, and yet he acted as if he was oblivious to the merit of Colletti's position.

Boras was tacitly threatening that if the Dodgers didn't sweeten the deal on their own, Ramirez would play for the first team that did improve on that offer, or for the highest bidder.

In other words, the Dodgers would have had one bite at the apple, and they'd be denied a second chance to improve their offer later.

Is that completely rational?

Not really, but who said negotiation is ever 100 percent reasonable or predictable?

As it turned out, no other team stepped up with a better deal, and Manny had to accept what was on the table.

. . . .

Best Practice 42
Salespeople Should Bargain for Big Salaries

A few years ago, I published an article touting the glories of being paid on a straight commission basis if you are a salesperson.

Among other things, I pointed out that the upside can be tremendous, if you are effective in the art of persuasion. Typically, you'll be paid for your results, meaning you can receive what you're worth, which is very gratifying, financially and emotionally.

But I've had cause to change my mind. Boom times never last, and just when we think they will, money gets tight. As we saw in the Great Recession, economies can change almost overnight. Furthermore, access to credit for both businesses and individuals is restricted by tight-fisted lending practices. Cash is king, and a bird in hand is worth several in the bush.

This means if you sell for someone else, *you should negotiate the biggest guaranteed salary you should get*. This is always a good practice in any economy, but when money tightens, it is even more essential to be paid up front. Here's my reasoning. In harder times:

1. Spending is cut across the economy, so you're probably going to make fewer sales.
2. Companies are likely to cut back on the generosity of their commission plans, making your pay envelopes thinner.
3. It will take longer to open and close deals, even when pursuing superqualified buyers.

All of this means that if you accept a commission-only post, you will have to self-finance.

Another good reason to be more salaried than commissioned is that when companies are fronting you money, they have sunk costs into you. They run the risk of losing these funds if they don't give you other forms of support, especially *good leads* that you can turn into orders. They can easily cut back on these expensive leads if you're commissioned, but they'll think twice if you are salaried.

In short, if you are a salesperson, you should go to some form of a salary, either in a draw against commissions or as a salary plus commissions.

In addition, you should bargain, if you can, for more frequent pay periods. In a small business or mom-and-pop situation, you can probably get paid weekly. I see some ads that will pay salespeople daily, and in a banana-peel-like economy, that won't seem flaky; it will look good!

. . . .

Best Practice 43
Beware of Sluggish Negotiations

I am probably one of the few students of bargaining who take an ultraserious look at what occurs *after* official negotiations have concluded.

I'm interested in the impact of the negotiation process on the participants, especially when they were dickering for human services and the negotiations were stretched beyond the customary time limits.

To go back to Manny Ramirez (Best Practice 41), he and the Dodgers came to terms for a two-year deal, cancelable after one year, at Manny's discretion.

The agreement capped several months of uncertainty, and mutual accusations leaked to the press. All of these spanned the economic funk that shrouded the planet between October 2008 and March 2009.

Still, a deal was cut, so all was well that ended well, right?

Not really, because Manny pulled up lame in spring training, nursing a strained hamstring muscle. That can happen to anybody. What's so special in this case?

I contend that Manny's protracted negotiations affected his physical fitness. Had he been signed earlier, he wouldn't be rushing to get into shape, placing undue strains on a body that was rapidly aging and relatively idle during the off-season.

Dodgers manager Joe Torre was reluctant to use his star player during preseason games. Thus this premier hitter didn't get in nearly the same number of at-bats or fielding experience he was used to getting, exacerbating his lack of preparedness.

By Manny's own estimate, he was playing at 50 percent effectiveness on opening day.

As negotiation pundits, how do we analyze this phenomenon?

I think we have to see negotiations that drag on as incurring hidden additional costs that are not otherwise factored into deals.

The Dodgers were officially paying Manny $45 million for two years. In reality, as the season started, they were paying this money to a 50 percent effective Manny.

I don't think this is what the Dodgers deliberately bargained for. For his part, Manny didn't want to be limping along, not contributing, not showcasing his talents, disabling him from sweetening his contract at season's end.

In the end, Manny was traded to the White Sox, and he was not renewed by that club. So the Dodgers deal was really a lose-lose proposition for the slugger.

The moral?

Beware of negotiations that limp along. You can only stretch them so far before they hamstring you.

. . . .

Best Practice 44
When a No Is as Good as a Yes

There are some very decent negotiation books on the market. *Getting to Yes* is a stalwart, and *Getting Past No* is a sequel.

But sometimes, with people that are dour, negative, and taciturn, it pays to promote a negative reply as a shortcut to negotiating your way to an ultimate yes.

For example, I just left a phone conversation with a fellow who works for an investment firm. I was negotiating with him for information, specifically for the best way to get in touch with the president of his company.

Because his first instinct is to say no, to deny me access to the head honcho, I realize it would be nearly impossible to get him to say yes in this circumstance.

He doesn't know me, and there's no upside for him unless I manufacture one.

Which is what I did, on the spot. Here's how I got the information I needed.

"I have a personal question for you, Dave." I began. "If I could show you how to make a lot more money, at absolutely no cost to you, you wouldn't turn that down, would you?"

"No."

"That's what I'm going to talk to the president about. What's the best way to get his attention?"

"Oh, OK. I suggest you email him."

And then he promptly surrendered the otherwise confidential email address of the person who can retain me and cut a check for my consulting services.

You've heard of yes-men and women, right? When you're selling and negotiating, you'll find a lot more no-folks.

Don't try to get them to jump, whistle, and volunteer information all at the same time. They're not practiced in it, nor are they remotely inclined to help you.

Go with the flow, or in this case with the blockage.

Engineer your conversations so that your counterparts can comfortably and reflexively say no, no, and no for as many times as it takes for you to get exactly what you want.

. . . .

Best Practice 45
Get a Third Party to Pay

I was competing neck and neck against a division of Xerox for a national training deal with an airline.

Thinking I had a leg up because I had just concluded a successful national sales training program for the same airline, I was optimistic. But I lost out.

When I asked my contact why he decided to go with Xerox, he replied:

"They asked me a really good question that I couldn't answer: 'Goodman is good, but he's a small outfit; What if he dies in the middle of the contract?'"

At the time, all I could weakly offer is the fact that I haven't died in the middle of a job yet, and I was a young guy in great health.

Later I would learn that the possibility of my death or disablement was an insurable risk. My client or I could have purchased a policy to compensate them in the event of my untimely demise. Considering that I am a stout individual, it would have been cheap to buy.

In other words, I could have brought in a third party to assume part of the burden, in this case to "pay" for the contingency that I might not perform.

Every negotiator should be aware of spins on this possibility. Let's say I want to sell a training program to a company in Chicago, but they can't afford my asking price.

They might be open to having me invite a second company, a noncompetitor, to send people to the same program, defraying part of the cost. Or if I want to address members of a trade association, I might find an advertiser or sponsor who could subsidize the event out of its marketing budget in trade for placing its name prominently on my training materials, while also giving it the opportunity to introduce me to the group.

Doing something for A while getting B to pay is a brilliant way to create win–win–win deals.

Frequently, realtors will part with some of their commissions in one way or another to close the gap between an asked-for price and an offered price.

Ask yourself, "Who else can I get to chip in?"

Sometimes entire businesses are built on this concept. It has been reported that many for-profit vocational colleges have prospered because they offer financial aid. For one publicly traded firm, 96 percent of the tuition is being paid by the U.S. government in the form of student loans. Just another example of getting a third party to pay!

· · · · · · · · · · · · · ·

Best Practice 46
Avoid Five Traps in Preparing for a Negotiation

The most irksome, nasty, peevish, and stingy negotiator in creation resides between your two ears.

It's you, and of course it's me too.

We are our own worst enemies in a negotiation because we fall into five traps:

1. We remain in our own heads instead of seeing the world from our counterpart's viewpoint. As I demonstrate in my negotiation classes, ferreting out the other party's options and opinions pays off nicely.

2. We fail to set goals before entering a negotiation. Fred had his eye on a new grand piano, and after doing his research he boiled his choices down to two: a Suzuki and a Yamaha. He called and visited lots of Yamaha dealers, but they were hesitant to discount the model he wanted. The Suzuki, reportedly a fine instrument as well, wasn't in the same class, but Fred was willing to settle for it, mostly because it priced out 20 percent less than its rival. Still not convinced he wanted the Suzuki, Fred happened upon a one-

day sale of Yamahas at Costco. Noting the price was discounted by about $2,000 from what he had seen at dealers, he instantly bought the model he wanted.

What does this have to do with negotiation? Fred got them to throw in free delivery and setup, but apart from that, he simply accepted the price as offered. Still, he negotiated the terms he wanted most with *himself.* He wanted a Yamaha at a slightly higher price than a Suzuki. When he found that exact deal, he grabbed it. He had already established their relative values, but more significantly, he had determined their respective values *to him.* Sale prices are great, and smart negotiators are prepared to snatch them when they come along.

3. We're impatient. Instead of starting with the assumption that no deal is better than a bad one, we endorse the concept that *some* deal is better than none. Be willing to walk away, and establish your walkaway price in advance.

4. We dislike negotiating, believing it is beneath us. That is a prescription for failure, because in many cultures negotiating is promoted and perfectly normal, and in some cases it appears insulting to be *unwilling* to bargain at least a little.

5. We believe other people's prices to be fair, objective, and scientifically derived. But pricing is more of an art than a science, and most pricing errs on the side of packing in too much profit instead of too little. So there's "water" in most prices, and our job as smart negotiators is to flush it out.

. . . .

Best Practice 47
Try Shrugging

Here's a practice that pundit Herb Cohen swears by.

Somebody makes you an offer that is so low, such a shock, and so upsetting that you don't know where to begin to respond.

Or a person makes a perfectly suitable first offer, which is in the range of acceptability, given what you've plotted in advance.

These seem to be dramatically disparate scenarios that would evoke entirely different responses from you, correct?

In the first situation, you'd be inclined to say "Get outta here!" or "You must think I'm crazy!"

And in the second, you'd be tempted to tip your hand, to confess, "I was looking for something a little higher."

But what if I told you that one of the best initial gambits *in either circumstance is to do the same thing?*

What's more, would you be surprised if I recommended saying nothing at all, and instead simply shrugging while raising your palms upward toward the ceiling?

This "What gives?" response accomplishes a number of things:

1. You avoid making a counteroffer. If you counter their figure, chances are you'll compromise your position and make unnecessary concessions.

2. You provide feedback that says, "You'll need to do better than that!" but it is more powerful to send this

message nonverbally. If you just say the other party needs to do better, a savvy negotiator can elicit a number from you by simply repeating your key word as a question: "Better?"

3. It's less offensive and more low-key to use gestures at this point. It says, "I'm confused; tell me more." If your counterpart tells more, inevitably he'll reveal more too, giving you valuable information. Second, it provides just enough aversive feedback to motivate the other person to cut to the chase, to skip small improvements in the offer and to make larger ones. Plus, a shrug makes him monitor your body language and try to make you more comfortable. By trying to put you at ease, he gets hooked on the need to please.

This is such a simple move that you have to wonder if it will work. It does, because while most people are trained to haggle with their jaws, they're utterly unschooled in bartering with their shoulders.

. . . .

Best Practice 48
Beware of Any "Standard" Agreement

One of my readers, a commission salesman, sent me a question that I've been asked several times: what percentage is the industry standard when it comes to negotiating sales commissions?

I'll share with you my response to him, and I hope it gives you some guidance for negotiating compensation.

Your sales commission is a truly negotiable item. Just as there are no "standard" contracts (though every stationery store sells documents with that header), there are no hard-and-fast rules regarding straight commission compensation.

I have seen 20 percent a great deal, but this will vary based on a lot of factors:

How well known is the product?
What is the profit margin?
How long does it take to make a sale?
How difficult is this item to sell?

You need to be careful with any plan, especially if you're selling for someone else.

Make sure that *someone on staff now* is making great money. Ask that person to confide in you, telling you that management (1) pays on time and (2) has no history of cutting back on the commission structure.

Make sure that management does not keep more than a 10 percent reserve against chargebacks, if they compute them at all. It also needs to be explicitly agreed that funds that accumulate in a chargeback reserve are yours, to be released to you at a definite point in time, such as sixty days after sale or upon receipt of payment from the client.

Be on your guard whenever you see a proposal or a contract that has the word *standard* in its heading. It is put there for the precise purpose of discouraging negotiation.

. . . .

Best Practice 49
Offer Something Cheap to You, Yet Precious to Them

There is a lot of room for creativity in negotiating, but few people pay attention to the possibilities. If you do, you can turn what would have been a busted deal into a great one.

For example, when I was consulting for a major airline, my contact wanted me to do a nationwide training program for his field sales reps. He also wanted to pay less than the going rate for my services.

Typically I eschew these proposals, because my rates are more than fair, and they represent my unique skills and proven track record. But Tom was creative. He thought he could pay me less and more at the same time, which, as you might imagine, is quite a trick.

He offered about 50 percent less money than I wanted, but he threw in a piece of plastic that may have cost his company a buck or two. It was a consultant's identification card. It enabled me to be admitted to his company's locations, but Tom promised it could also open other doors around the world. By flashing that card, I could save 50 percent or more on first-class hotels. I traveled a lot, so this would mean I could stay at a Hilton on a Hampton Inn budget.

This card would make my life easier as a business traveler, and the dollar value over time could exceed many thousands of dollars, Tom maintained. I bought his argument and uncharacteristically reduced my fee after he threw in a few more perks.

What Tom did well was to ask, "What do I have to offer that is almost free to me, but of great potential value to him?"

His answer saved our deal, or at any rate made it a very good one for both of us.

How much was that card worth to me? Over $150,000, by my estimate!

. . . .

Best Practice 50
Metacommunicate!

Gamesmanship, egos, and the exhilaration of trying to come up with a big victory can easily ruin a negotiation. But you can put things right by commenting on the progress of the negotiation itself.

This gambit is called *metacommunication*, and research indicates that it is sometimes the only way to get a failing encounter back on track.

Metacommunication is defined as talking about the way we're talking, with the goal of improving our communication.

For example, you might say: "I'm afraid we're getting a little too loud here, and I'm not able to focus on the underlying problem, so if we can tone it down a little, I'd appreciate it, and I think we'll get more done."

Or if the session is humming along, you might praise your collective work: "I'm pleased we're making progress.

If we keep going at this rate, we might be able to finish by noon."

This keeps the wheels greased, while potentially preventing any backsliding or sudden resistance.

Once more, metacommunication is talking about the way we're talking. You should try this in your negotiations to keep them moving forward or to get them back onto the rails.

. . . .

Best Practice 51
Play the Shell Game and Win

As I write this, there is an avid discussion in progress at a blog for consultants. The question is: "How much does the average practitioner charge?"

I've never positioned myself as average, so I'm not terribly interested in competing with the fictional thought of as an "average consultant." But I have been used by other consultants who wanted to make their fees seem reasonable. One of them, a chap I had actually trained in Ohio, used to quote a figure to his prospects of $1,200 per day, which was less than the prevailing average charged by those in my field. Then he'd urge his potential clients to comparison-shop by calling me in California, posing as people interested in my services.

I'd recite fees that were at least two or three times what he quoted. Adding travel expenses, my costs would seem steep indeed, making his seem like a bargain.

He confessed this chicanery to me one day when we were chatting over the phone.

I wondered aloud, "How can you charge only $1,200 per day and survive?"

He asked me, "What proportion of your consulting is done off-site, versus on-site, at the client's place of business?"

"About 80 percent on-site, 20 percent off," I responded.

"For me, it's the reverse," he explained. He went on to inform me that he would be able to sell sixty to ninety billable days per month as a result, whereas I could sell twenty at most. Besides, I'd exhaust myself traveling.

He'd double- and triple-bill his clients, selling the same calendar day two and three times. If he was doing a workbook that took a day to compose, he'd bill for five days.

In other words, because our prospects are so fixated on comparison-shopping based on daily billing rates, he deliberately decided to turn that to his advantage. He quoted one-third my rate, but sold three times as many, or more, billable days. We were effectively charging the same amount—or he was actually charging more than me—but he appeared to be significantly cheaper.

By the way, what is a "billable day?" Is it 6, 8, 10, 12 or 18 hours? Is there a standard? I don't think so.

Recently I departed from a client's site at 12:30 p.m. EST and headed to the airport for a 2:30 flight. I caught it and connected in Dallas–Fort Worth to Los Angeles.

I took a shared van home and arrived at 11:30 PST that night.

My day began at the hotel at 7 a.m. EST, because I was prepping for my 8:30 arrival at the site. I ended at 2:30 in the next morning, EST. How long was that consulting day? Nineteen and a half hours?

Now get this: That client chastised me, somewhat impishly, about the half-day I was giving him on Friday, conveniently overlooking how that half-day was really two-and-a-half days of clock time.

This is the *shell game*, played from the client's point of view. If you think it is rare, think again.

Today computer printers are supercheap to buy. The reason is that manufacturers are making their money on replacement ink cartridges, which are getting more and more expensive.

Gillette made his fortune playing the same game—giving away shavers that would only be functional with the replacement blades his company sold. While people were fixated on getting a free razor, he was locking them into buying his specially fitted blades.

Attorneys might charge three billable hours for composing a letter that is mostly boilerplate, requiring twenty minutes to customize (if it was done by the attorney at all and not by a paralegal). Of course, attorneys must have the education, judgment, and wisdom to select the best letter for the client and circumstances, but they would find it difficult to send out a statement with the category "Education, Judgment, and Wisdom," on it and expect to receive $600 or $1000 for that.

It's easier to bill, and seem to be paid, "hourly."

I'm a professional keynote speaker, appearing at conferences and conventions worldwide. Some clients have what I consider unrealistically miniscule speaker budgets. It could take me a business week to prepare for, travel to, speak at, return from, and recuperate from an engagement in Europe or in Latin America.

I need to be compensated for those seven days, yet some clients want to pay only for the on-site time. Still, we can make a deal, providing they play the shell game with me.

Often they'll have substantial separate "educational materials" budgets, and they'll gladly purchase scores if not hundreds of my audiovisual programs for attendees. Plus, they may be amenable to providing me with first-class or business-class airfare. They may be able to contract not only for a keynote, but also for breakout workshops, for which I would be paid separately, while I'm at the scene.

Voilà! I can give them a great deal on my keynote speaking fee, providing they purchase the other items on the menu.

This is yet another version of the shell game.

Play it, and win in your negotiations!

. . . .

Best Practice 52
Learn How to Beat the Car Business

I learned a ton about the car business by working as an account executive for a Beverly Hills leasing company.

The president of our firm had a heart-to-heart chat with me one day. He asked me a crucial question: "Gary, what is a person's greatest expense over the course of a lifetime?"

"A house?" I guessed.

"No, it's buying, maintaining, insuring, and selling automobiles. Houses are often good investments, appreciating over the long haul, but cars are outright expenses," he explained.

For this reason, it pays to learn something about car values before you buy or sell one.

While some things have changed since I was in the car business (especially the relative popularity of leasing versus buying), most things haven't. And there's one key metric that you and I and everyone who drives should watch very carefully: a car's residual value.

Residual or resale value is what a car is expected to be worth after a given period of time, such as 24 or 36 months. Leasing companies try to predict this figure this with precision, because a car's monthly payment will be greatly impacted by its anticipated market appeal down the road.

Let's say you're looking at two cars, each of which is priced at $24,000. Which one will be worth more by the time you get around to selling it or returning it to the leasing company?

If Car A is worth only $12,000 after 36 months, while Car B will fetch $15,000, you'll pay for the $3,000 difference over the course of your lease. When you factor in the cost of money, that is, interest, you'll pay up to $100 more per month to drive the car that will bring $3,000 less as a used car three years later.

Another way of putting it is to say you can lease a lot better car for the same money if you choose a more desirable model.

Example: recently Mark priced out various leases on a Ford Mustang convertible. He was quoted $390–$550 per month, depending on the model and the lease's term.

Shopping around, he found he could lease a Mercedes CLK 350 convertible for 27 months, with even more optional equipment, for only $595 per month, including scheduled maintenance. Yes, there was a slightly larger drive-off to be paid, but he was able to get a $58,000 ride roughly for the price of a $38,000 vehicle.

Granted, there was special manufacturer financing available on the Mercedes, but the difference is still dramatic, and much of it is attributable to the way this car is expected to hold up in the marketplace.

Apart from maintenance, the actual cost to you for a car that is under warranty is mainly based on three things: (1) the initial price of the vehicle; (2) financing; and (3) residual value.

Most people study the first two very carefully but ignore the third, but as you can see, it is critical.

How can you predict the resale value two years down the road? Take a hint from leasing companies. Look at what the same model has done during the past two or three years, and use the same percentage of depreciation as the predicted rate for today's new cars.

What if you're considering a brand-new model that doesn't have two years or more of history in the marketplace? That's more challenging. Leasing companies tend to use conservative percentages, saying, for instance, that today's new model will bring 65 percent of its initial cost 30 months later, but this is just a guess.

There are always surprises. If your car fares better than the average, you'll have some happy choices: you can (1) exchange it for a new lease sooner than you might have planned, (2) sell it for more money, or (3) keep driving it, knowing it is a good store of value.

On the other hand, if your car is dropping in value like a stone, you might consider dumping it right away for a better-performing model, or resigning yourself to keeping it for a very long time, after which residual value becomes so low that it is a negligible factor in your decision making.

One more tip: residual value, as determined by Kelley Blue Book, typically takes a big hit just before the new year's vehicles come out, especially if there is a redesign of the body on a particular model, making older versions appear dated.

So if you're thinking of selling or trading in, try to do it at least 60–90 days before the new ones hit the showrooms.

Want to beat the car business? *"Buy the best car you can afford, maintain it, and keep it forever,"* my boss smiled.

. . . .

Best Practice 53
Negotiate like a Child

When I was consulting for a major mutual fund company, one of my contacts described in the compass of two words how her employees could wrap her around their little fingers:

"Whining *works!*" she said, with some exasperation.

Whining, throwing tantrums, refusing to play nicely with others, and pouting are generally considered to have no proper place in business. But that doesn't mean they aren't used quite successfully in the 9-5 world.

Consider the example of one bad boy I encountered at a software company. He wanted his own large, private space away from others. But instead of earning the corner office through years of toil, he decided on a shortcut. He quite loudly communicated with clients over the phone, irritating his cellmates—sorry, I mean his cube mates.

Hopelessly distracted, they complained to management. His superiors spoke to him, and he loudly replied, "That's JUST HOW I TALK, I GUESS!"

He got his corner office in short order, complete with a sound-muffling door, bypassing the requirement of paying his dues and receiving the typical sequence of promotions.

He was 100 percent aware of the effects he had on others, and his loudness was simply a negotiation ploy that worked.

Bill Adler Jr. published a book in 2006 titled *How to Negotiate like a Child: Unleash the Little Monster Within to Get Everything You Want.*

Some of his gambits include:

"Take your toys and go home."

"Worry the other side that you might be sick."

"Ask the person who's most inclined to say yes."

Hey, if you've been a kid or you've spawned some, you're sure to recognize some of these tactics. If you don't, you've been playing in the wrong sandbox!

. . . .

Best Practice 54
Beware of Garbage Charges

Most businesses seek some sort of advantage so they can justify charging premium prices.

I encountered a company that tried to *double* its billable rate by invoking just one word, and I'm sure its people get away with this ruse all the time.

But let's back up to when my kitchen sink backed up.

I tried to chuck a pasta sauce that I must have made with too much tomato paste. Besides giving myself heartburn, I got a nasty surprise when I tried to dispose of my monstrous creation. Just when I thought I got rid of the ooze, it, like any great villain, gurgled back to life, filling both sections of my sink.

At 7:30 in the morning, I called a plumber I had used in the past. Actually, I had to call twice, because he didn't respond to my first plea for help.

The technician phoned and promised a visit some five hours later, at 1 p.m. About 2:30, I had to phone him again. Where was he?

"I'm finishing up a job in Beverly Hills, and I'll be there in an hour. By the way, you know our rate for emergency service is $195 plus another $195, and then we go from there."

"What?"

He repeated the words.

I had to probe further. "Is this a double rate because it's a Saturday?"

"No, it's because it's an emergency."

No pipes had burst. There wasn't a geyser shooting a hundred feet in the air in my front yard. I wasn't knee-deep in rising water.

But he was telling me that his response, requiring no less than one full working day from my initial call, somehow qualified as an emergency.

"Hey," I said, "I'm just happy you're not a surgeon or a paramedic. If they handled emergencies the way you do, I'd be long dead!"

I looked up an alternative company. Their fee: $94.05, and they even showed up within the promised half-hour.

Not once did they use the *emergency* word. They just went about their business in a quick, professional manner, charging a reasonable price.

Pay close attention to how companies define various classes of service. You could be routed into paying twice as much you should simply by the slick insertion of a single word.

. . . .

Best Practice 55
Always Leave Yourself an Out

Many of us enter into negotiations with *too much* authority to make deals, and then we use it, often without reservation. We agree to terms that a few hours later seem very unfavorable, but by that point we feel that we must live up to our word and the deal cannot be undone.

Or can it?

If we leave ourselves an out, we can get out of bad or disadvantageous deals without incurring a loss.

What's a typical out?

"I'm going to have to run this by our legal department for their stamp of approval" is a typical out in the corporate sphere.

"I need to consult my spouse" is certainly a time-tested, tried-and-true out in our personal lives.

We see outs in real estate contracts that enable a buyer to approve of the reports submitted by termite, roofing, and plumbing inspectors. If it turns out there is a lot of decay or damage, typically purchasers can walk away or insist on major price concessions from the seller.

I think of outs as providing cooling-off periods—intervals in which we can walk ourselves back through the terms of a deal. If it seems unfair, lopsided, or at all imprudent, we have reserved the right to say, "Sorry, but I changed my mind."

Hint: leave yourself as much latitude as you can when drafting your out. The best language starts with, "The purchaser reserves the right to cancel this agreement within forty-eight hours for any reason."

Any is the operative term in the last sentence. If the buyer has a bad dream about the transaction, that's an out. If he has *any* misgivings for *any* reason that might seem absolutely stupid to every other person on the planet, it doesn't matter. He can reconsider. It doesn't mean he will, nor does it portend he'll opt out. But he has the power to do so, without penalty.

Always negotiate the most generous out you can. And by generous, I mean to you, of course!

. . . .

Best Practice 56
If You Make a Concession, Get a Concession

We've all heard of the Golden Rule, which means we should do unto others as we would have them do unto us.

This sentiment is reflected in several sayings that promote reciprocity. "One hand washes the other" comes to mind.

Reciprocity is a part of civilized conduct, but many of us forget this fundamental fact when we negotiate. Instead of giving and taking, we permit our counterparts to take and to take without returning the favor.

They say: "I'm going to need X," and we say, "OK."

They follow this with "And I'm also going to need Y."

"Fair enough," we chime in, and before our tongues stop wagging they say, "And Z will have to come with that as well."

"Hmm, you drive a hard bargain, but, sure, why not?" we respond.

What's wrong with this picture?

Negotiation is a value-for-value exchange. But the way this dialogue is going, we're not *exchanging*. We're capitulating, conceding one deal point after the next.

Here's a Best Practice you should always try to invoke: *when you make a concession, get one in return.*

The easiest way to do this is to say, "Yes, I'll give you X, and in return I'll need A."

The *yes-and* approach is almost a sure winner, because it seems only normal to link the satisfaction of their want with the satisfaction of your want.

What happens if we don't say yes-and? We'll concede, concede, and concede again, seemingly without end. That's not negotiating; it's surrendering.

. . . .

Best Practice 57
If A Offends You, Twist B's Arm

I had a terrible time getting my new washer-dryer repaired under warranty by a major retailer.

Because of a persistent electronic problem, it broke three or four times during the year. One would think they'd swap machines to spare themselves from continuously dispatching fixers to my home and to retain me as a customer. But they didn't, and with each repair call I made, the longer it took for them to even set an appointment.

I complained to them directly, online and by phone, to no avail.

Then I expanded the battlefield.

The offending firm is part of a conglomerate, consisting of a major appliance manufacturing unit and thousands of retail stores. They have a huge Internet presence. The parent company also owns a mail-order clothing firm with which I have done considerable trade.

I decided to boycott the clothing unit because the washing machine was not repaired correctly.

"Why punish B when A is the culprit?" you might wonder.

By putting pressure on all business units, we increase the odds of getting what we need from the one that is callous, indifferent to our needs. We embarrass them in front of their peers, and one pressures the next to reform.

In a book titled *Satisfaction,* J. D. Power IV discusses customers who become "assassins." They have been so offended by poor treatment that they go out of their way to create payback. Power says assassins are "50 percent more likely to tell someone about a bad experience than an advocate is to tell someone about a great experience."

I teach companies how to improve their sales and service processes, and I'd like to think in my modest way I'm raising the stakes on behalf of all consumers when companies offend us.

My recommendation: Don't punish just one business unit. Go after them all, every evil twin and remote corporate family member you can find.

If A offends you, twist B's arm to negotiate better customer service. It's not assassination, and it isn't bullying. It's simply finding more leverage to get the benefits of timely and capable warranty service.

. . . .

Best Practice 58
Take the Gamble out of Your Negotiations

Barely twenty-one years old, I had just placed a foolishly large blackjack bet at a Lake Tahoe casino. The lonely column of chips in front of me represented my net worth. This was going to be my last hand, one way or another.

The dealer fanned the cards around the table.

Oh, no! He drew an ace as his up card!

I felt flush in the face, embarrassed I had stuck it out at that table for so many losing hands in a row.

Expecting the worst, I looked at my cards.

I held two jacks, which in most circumstances would at least give me a draw if not an outright win.

He peered at his down card.

"Insurance?" he asked, gazing at each player in turn.

I had been taught that insurance is a sucker's bet. You ante up more cash on a bad hand that is not worth protecting, and the dealer still beats you, with or without hitting 21.

But this time, instead of reflexively declining the coverage and the additional premium I would have to pay for it, I looked at him and starkly asked: *"What do you suggest?"*

After a two-second pause that seemed to spread a sound-deadening vapor throughout the casino, permitting only him and I to hear each other, he said, *"Take it!"*

Would he lie to me? Was he actually admitting he held a ten beneath that ace, that he was on the verge of busting me out if I didn't accept the offer?

I bought the insurance. He had blackjack. I recovered my bet.

Tossing him a serious tip, I gratefully left the table.

This wasn't a gaming episode, though by all outward appearances it seemed to be. It was a negotiation, demonstrating that the most important thing your counterpart has isn't power or money or more options than you have.

He has *information* that is critical to your success. If you can get him to disclose it, you'll come up a winner.

Sometimes it's just a matter of asking, though that's the last thing we do. We disable ourselves by thinking, "He'd never tell me that!" or "It's against his interest to make such a disclosure!"

You'd be surprised, as I was when that dealer helped me out. Remember, the only sure way to take the gamble out of negotiating is to get the information that is unavailable to you. Don't ever be afraid to ask.

Here's even more dramatic confirmation of this principle.

A consulting guru I knew ran seminars around the country at the same time I was touring with mine. We stumbled upon each other at the Hyatt Regency Cambridge one morning, and we agreed to have lunch after we returned to California.

On the appointed day, I ventured to a restaurant close to his office. We had a nice meal, and as I recall, I picked up the check. As we were heading to the parking lot, I asked Howard a very simple question.

"I've noticed you sell audios as alternative purchases for people that can't attend your live seminars. How does that work for you?"

"It pays for the ads!" he beamed with the sort of pride you only find in those that have struck gold.

From that point, I started offering the same deal to those that couldn't attend my college-sponsored seminars. At one school, our mailing of 100,000 pieces was late in getting posted, so the first few venues on our Midwestern tour were undersubscribed.

No problem, as it turned out. This booboo induced lots of folks to buy my audios instead, for which I had negotiated a handsome profit margin.

Those proceeds helped me to scrape together a down payment for my first home.

Remember that lunch with Howard? From my standpoint, the entire purpose was to learn how lucrative it is to vend audios.

I got the one piece of information he had that I was missing, and it bought me a house!

Again, ask and often enough you will receive. You too can come up aces.

. . . .

Best Practice 59
Exploit Nonverbal Cues and Clues

There is a painting in Pasadena's Norton Simon Museum that presents a portrait of a gentleman, or so we would think at a cursory glance.

But the artist must have been slightly miffed at his subject. Perhaps the patron was less than generous, or possibly he was late in paying previous commissions.

Nothing about the subject's facial expression, clothing, or posture reveals the artist's contempt. However, if you start from the bottom of the frame and move up, focusing on the subject's fingers, and, more to the point, on his fingernails, you'll detect what I'm referring to.

There are traces of trapped dirt that are barely visible to the attentive eye. The artist took pains to put them there, and in doing so delivered a completely accurate image of the man from the painter's vantage point. Hundreds of years later, this silent editorial continues to whisper: "See, this is no gentleman!"

Erving Goffman, a famous sociologist, noted that in human communication there are two types of messages. He called the first "expressions given."

Let's say you're speaking from a manuscript before a public gathering. You'd be giving an explicit message tailored to produce a specific result in the audience. Likewise, if you're a salesperson and you follow a set presentation, you are mainly concerned about crafting and delivering an expression given.

But Goffman pointed out that there are also "expressions given off." These are inadvertent messages that we send. They seem to have lives of their own.

In the legendary Kennedy-Nixon presidential debates, a sweating Nixon gave off to the TV audience the impression of a man who wasn't cool under pressure—someone less presidential than Kennedy, at least to many viewers. Some say this gaffe cost him the election.

In communicating, and especially when negotiating, it pays to listen to the whole person. This involves monitoring what they say, when they say it, how they say it, and above all, what they *don't* say, or what their bodies reveal that contradicts their expressions given.

The negotiator who speaks very slowly, or who says he has all of the time in the world to make or not to make a deal, gives himself away by checking his watch too often and by asking too many "when" questions.

Gamblers know that their counterparts are inclined to give off "tells" that reveal the quality of their poker hands. For instance, they might scratch their noses, tap their fingers on the table, or take a large in breath after glancing at their down cards.

In the James Bond movie *Casino Royale*, the villain is perceived to have done just this—or did he? Savvy gamblers and negotiators give "false tells" on purpose to sucker their foes into making catastrophic mistakes. Some are so adept that they can get away with a lot.

I was negotiating the sale of a piece of real estate, and I met the buyer, along with one of his workmen, at the property. He spent a considerable amount of time deriding the place, mentioning every flaw and shortcoming. Then he made his offer, with utter seriousness, in a flat "Take it or leave it" tone.

I thought he was being sincere, but my Doberman had a different impression.

He growled within a few seconds of hearing the "offer."

"Is he growling at me?" my counterpart asked, obviously shaken by Blue's intrusion into the deal.

"Gee, I don't know," I replied.

Obviously, the guy gave off something that was there, but I wasn't perceptive enough to pick it up. Nonetheless, I trusted Blue's assessment, and told the guy I'd think over his offer.

Within two weeks, I sold the place for substantially more than this fellow offered.

What's the moral to the story?

Bring a Doberman to all of your negotiations!

Seriously, train yourself to listen to the whole person and to pick up on clues that you've probably been ignoring.

Not only will you become a better communicator, but you'll get better results in your negotiations.

. . . .

Best Practice 60
Signal That You Need the Deal Less Than They Do

Some of the most pathetic folks are those who are in love with people who don't love them back.

If we're honest and we think back to our school days, all of us can recall being rebuffed at least once by the objects of our obsessions.

It's no fun, especially as we watch nonchalant men and women line up date after date with the most desirable people.

It's not fair!

We're trying so hard and getting nothing, while they're not trying at all and they're getting everything!

Exactly, and this is one of the essential truths about negotiating, whether it is for affection or for jobs, perks, or the best contractual terms.

Above all, repeat this to yourself the second you start to *really need* a specific outcome:

"He or she who wants the deal more loses!"

I had just bought a great pair of crocodile cowboy boots on the famous Sunset Strip. I couldn't have been happier with them, though they cost me many greenbacks.

A day or two later, as I was driving on Beverly Boulevard, I saw a "Cowboy Boots Sale!" sign leaning against what can only be called a shack.

Surrounded by chic designer stores, this wart was particularly conspicuous. I had to stop, just out of curiosity. Imagine how shocked I was when I saw a great collection of boots, including one of the styles I had declined, but still wanted, when I bought mine.

The proprietor was decked out in cowboy gear and turquoise rings, and was watching a dusty TV.

I did my best John Wayne impression as I said, "Howdy," and he smiled. To make a long story short, I walked out with three more sets of boots, for which I paid a mere fraction of their value. And I'm really happy with them and wear them every day I can.

How did I do so well?

He wanted to sell them much more than I needed to buy them. I showed him my new pair; he realized that I'm a true buyer and I didn't really need what he had. So when I offered a laughably small amount, he countered with a deal that was far better than I had ever hoped, and my results just improved from there.

In negotiations, the best thing is to not need the deal. But if you do, by all means, don't show it!

. . . .

Best Practice 61
Don't Be Snookered by Savvier Bargainers

Nobody likes to be snookered, especially when we're negotiating. It's especially painful if we're conned when dollars and cents are at stake.

Before you rush off to that next job interview or performance evaluation, or you race to bargain for that new car or enticing house, open your eyes and take the measure of the people you're negotiating with. It may save you money, embarrassment, and even your career.

Here are five tip-offs that they may be more skilled at the game than you are:

1. *Is he too dumb to be true?* The car dealer who seems to be the village idiot may be simply playing Columbo with you. You remember him—the TV detective who mumbled and bumbled his way to solving case after case, ensnaring the cockiest and most overconfident bad guys in the world.

   Playing the bozo is a smart move, according to a consensus of negotiating pros. By asking questions and appearing unsophisticated, you gain several advantages: you listen more than you talk, and you factfind and uncover their negotiating ranges. You also induce the other party to make damaging disclosures while avoiding the perils of blabbing.

   Exceptions exist, but they're rare. There was only one job interview where it paid for me to appear smart, and that was when I sought college teaching positions.

2. *Is she the nicest person you've met in months?* Nice people are disarming. They offer us a glass of water, hold doors open for us, smile, make pleasant eye contact, compliment our attire, and put us at ease. In doing so, they get far more from us, through our desire to reciprocate, than they would ever extract through bullying.

   The hard negotiator exists, the one who seems to put his bulldog personality before all else. But in most cases, he isn't nearly as effective as that flaw-lessly polite and congenial person that seems to *really like us*! Beware of them.

3. *Does she confess that she has limited authority?* This is one of the oldest gambits in the book. If I have lim-ited authority, I can't seal a deal all by myself; what "I think I might be able to do" is always tentative. If you, on the other hand, can seal the deal, what you promise is binding. This means you make conces-sions without a stop-loss, while I haven't conceded a thing. I'll leave the table with all of my options open, always promising to "see what I can do," but only getting final approval much later on, after you have caved in on point after point.

4. *Like a great football coach, does he know how to play the clock?* Effective negotiators seem to speed up and slow down the pace of the game at will. When a sense of urgency suits them, you feel pressure to answer their questions, provide commitments, and make conces-sions on the spot.

   When they find it valuable to slow the pace, to heighten your frustration and tweak your need for quick closure, suddenly they have to take a break, are called into another meeting, or have to take a call and get back to you later.

   The master of the clock is typically a negotiation master as well.

5. *Just when you think you have a deal, does she need just one small favor or additional item?* As detailed in Best Practice 14, a nibble is a tiny morsel that your coun-

terpart asks for just as, or even sometime after, you think your terms have been agreed upon and are final. The nibbling buyer says to the car dealer, "Of course, you're going to give me a full tank of gas, aren't you?"

Depending on the model, that can be a $50 nibble, or much more, if you're buying a Winnebago. Is any sane seller going to refuse, to watch his commission scamper away over a measly few dollars? Yes, some will—the ones who resent nibblers—but most won't.

Looking at the bright side, now you know five of the most typical negotiating gambits. Of course you can use them too when you encounter someone with even less training!

· · · · · · · · · · · · · ·

Best Practice 62
Want a Great Deal or a Great House?

Periodically, I interview car dealers, realtors, and various businesspeople to get their input for my negotiation seminars and corporate training programs.

A young realtor, whose dad has also been in the field for decades with a prominent firm, recently mentioned that it is paramount for buyers to have a talk with themselves before negotiating for properties.

"They need to get their priorities straight," she said with earnestness. If they get caught up in bargaining fever, she asks them point-blank:

"Do you want a good deal or do you want a great house?"

People can plunge themselves so deeply in dickering and trying to beat the other party that they forget negotiating is about optimizing as well as maximizing.

Sure, we want to save as much as we can, but what we really need is *value*.

Ask yourself the same question before house hunting.

What is my primary purpose? To find a livable, comfortable home that I'll be happy in for years? Or am I looking to flip houses, which speculators do when they try to find bargains, fix them up a little, and place them back onto the market at a profit?

Ideally, you want to get a great bargain on your dream house, but this is very unlikely. If it's that cool an abode, and the seller isn't desperate or dumb, you won't be alone in bidding for it.

I came across a professional home speculator. He specializes in repairing and restoring 1920s and 1930s Spanish-style homes in Southern California and then remarketing them. But when it came to his own house, his wife insisted they purchase a top-notch place, and he admits, "I paid full price for it."

Why?

"Making your wife happy is worth a lot!" he smiled.

If a purchase is going to make you happy, if it imparts value in the long run, then be satisfied. Sure, it's wonderful to knock a few dollars off an already attractive purchase, but don't always make this essential.

. . . .
Best Practice 63
Leave Them Feeling They Made a Great Deal

How effective are you when you're negotiating?

Perhaps you're like the young couple that sets out for the local car dealership. They want to spend no more than $12,000.

Seeing a sticker price within a few thousand of that, they start negotiating.

The dealer won't budge, but he asks: "Do you have a trade-in?"

Yes, it's been in a recent crash on the freeway, but still drivable. To them, it's ugly.

To the dealer, it's a little nugget of gold.

He knows he can get at least $6,000 just by selling the car for parts, so he offers them $3,500 for it. That's more than a used-car lot has offered, so they figure that when you add up everything—even if they pay close to the sticker price for the new car—they're doing slightly better than their $12,000 budget seemed to permit.

Everybody's happy. The dealer's made two good deals, and the customers think they've made one good one and one average one.

That's typical. Dealers always try to bundle two deals simultaneously. That way, they can seem generous with one and hold the line with the other. Still, they profit nicely.

But most importantly, *they leave customers thinking they're the ones who are smart negotiators and that they came out ahead.*

That winning feeling will make them come back again and again, and they'll even boast about their haggling abilities to their friends.

When you negotiate anything, it pays to make it seem to your counterparts that they've done really well. But this has to appear genuine and earned.

When I decided to buy a previously owned quality watch, I contacted a childhood friend who was in the jewelry business. She found what I wanted and recited a price. Having researched its retail value, which was significantly higher, I said OK without fanfare. I felt it was a good deal for both of us.

A few months later, at a social occasion, she remarked to me with no little consternation, "I lost my you-know-what on that deal!"

That struck me as phony. I didn't aggressively bargain at all, but she made it sound as if I extracted the price from her at the point of a gun. In retrospect, I think she was trying to make me feel that I got a great deal, but she went about it in a crass way that made her lose credibility.

Generally, if you have to do some work to knock down a quoted price, you will feel you've earned a bargain. That's one reason there is so much back-and-forth haggling at the car dealership, where the salesman has to check with his manager multiple times behind closed doors while keeping you in suspense. Often he's just out of sight, passing time and sipping coffee, so you'll feel you're making progress and earning your discount. The more you are made to struggle, the sweeter the ultimate concessions will seem to be, and the less you'll feel, after you drive away in style, that the outfit took advantage of you.

Of course, this all springs from basic human nature. We appreciate what we have to work for much more than what is merely handed to us. Also, our egos crave gratification—the feeling that we're smart, that we've matched wits with the pros and at least held our own. If they can make us feel we took advantage of them, we'll come running back to them time and again.

Now that takes real negotiation skill, don't you agree?

. . . .

Best Practice 64
Focus on Your Gains, Not Theirs

A couple was very interested in a beautiful designer glass house nestled in the foothills of Southern California.

Regarding himself as a tough and creative negotiator, the husband inserted into his otherwise decent offer an unusual clause that compelled the seller to pay closing costs.

Befuddled, and probably offended by this negotiating gambit, the seller decided that under no circumstances would she sell this dwelling to the couple. She disliked how they bargained.

Too often we gauge our results from a negotiation based on what we perceive the other party is getting from the deal. If we think they're asking for something they don't deserve, our mission shifts from getting what we need to preventing them from getting whatever it is, however minor, that they're demanding.

In this case, the seller just didn't want the couple to get the closing costs, which amounted to no more than 3 percent of the overall sales price. As it turned out, she discounted the property by 3 percent to the next couple that came along, in this case with a more conventional-sounding offer, and everybody walked away happy with their results.

Management guru Peter F. Drucker, my MBA professor for two and a half years, once said: "Our motivation depends less on what we're getting and more on what we believe others are getting." If we think they're profiting unfairly, then we automatically believe it is at our expense.

This is a major distraction in any negotiation. Often, as revealed by the real-estate transaction above, it is a deal killer.

By the way, after learning of their error, the first couple made a second offer to the seller, but it was too late.

· · · · · · · · · · · · ·

Best Practice 65
Determine if the Seller Is Motivated

Whatever you're negotiating, it is essential to gauge the urgency with which the other party wants or needs to make a deal.

When you're buying a piece of real estate, for example, one of the key questions to ask the listing broker is "How motivated is this seller?"

Usually you'll get an answer that will tell you something significant: (1) If the realtor balks or hesitates before answering, you can fairly safely surmise that the seller is not motivated, and neither is his agent, for that matter. In this case, where there is no urgency, you can't look forward to picking the property up at a bargain price or achieving any kind of deal quickly. (2) The most frequent reply is either "Very" or "She's motivated." Then you need to ask a simple question. Just repeat what the agent said: "She *is*?" This should be enough to induce the person to disclose some details, for instance, that the seller purchased a new home out of state, or that she is going through a major life event such as an empty nest or a divorce.

You can follow up these probes with another that I've found very useful: *when do you expect a price reduction?*

Again, this is a litmus test of the seller's motivation. While realtors are supposed to maintain a certain amount of confidentiality, face it: they're talkers, and they want to earn a commission, and the sooner the better.

Often they'll say: "I don't know if I should tell you this, but I think we might be seeing a reduction before too long."

Cool! Now you have confirmation that there is motivation.

Another pertinent question is: "How many offers have you had?"

You might be thinking, "They'll never tell me that!"

Wrong. Many of them will, and this is one more indication of a motivated seller.

By the way, all of this probing is a precursor to making an offer. If you don't see a string of green lights ahead, go no farther.

. . . .

Best Practice 66
Heat Up Sales with a Refrigerator Trick

A major benefit of being a full-time consultant is that you get a chance to learn an amazing amount about negotiation from your clients.

I was working with the owner of a large appliance store in Los Angeles, and he gave me a tutorial on the three grades of refrigerators. Each, of course, was separated from the other by price: about $250 in each grade. You could purchase an entry-level fridge at about $800, a middle grade at $1,050, and the top of the line started at around $1,300.

"Guess which one is most profitable to us?" he challenged.

"The most expensive, I suppose," I offered back.

"Wrong!" he beamed, obviously relishing his victory over the professional smart guy. "It's the middle grade, and can you guess which one most people end up buying?"

This time I was ready.

"The middle one?"

"Exactly," my client pointed out.

He went on to tell me that the most expensive model was the one that he made the least profit on, which, you have to admit, is counterintuitive. He also said, feature for feature, it was actually the best value for the customer and the most durable.

People like choices, he went on, and if you can offer three grades of anything, they'll gravitate to the middle because they think it's safe. They could do better or worse with regard to their investment, but the middle just feels right.

Remember this the next time you're negotiating. Don't just offer a high and a low.

Always include a most profitable middle choice!

. . . .

Best Practice 67
Don't Taunt a Dictator

Some negotiation gurus claim you can negotiate everything.

Perhaps, but you can't negotiate with everyone. And this constitutes a major problem.

Let's say it's time for your annual performance review, and your boss, who is also the owner of the company, declares he is going to award you a 5 percent raise in pay.

You think this is piddling, based on your achievements. What's more, you know that Mary down the hall, a far less meritorious worker, got 10 percent. Can you negotiate a better deal?

That depends on the overall rationality and good will of your boss. If he thinks you're challenging his judgment or being unappreciative, he may stonewall you and say, "Take it or leave it!"

In other words, if he insists on acting like a dictator and not a negotiator, then you're probably out of luck. Your only power is to quit your job, suffer the humiliation of unemployment, and, with a week or two of lost paychecks, possibly lose all of what you would have gained with a 10 percent raise.

In a word, your boss has *power*. It's not unlimited, but he has it in a significant enough supply to deny you what you want and perhaps to replace you with an even cheaper worker, who just might be in a developing country such as India or China.

What can you do?

You shouldn't argue that you deserve as much as Mary, for a few reasons. Pay is supposedly a confidential matter, and he'll be upset that it is being openly discussed. Mary will be rebuked for disclosing her raise, and you'll lose a potential ally and perhaps friend. Moreover, he won't like the collective bargaining tenor of your approach.

You can assert that you have done your best: you have beaten last year's performance, and you should be prepared to give him solid facts, statistics, and examples. You can also promise even better performance in the future, because a higher raise is both a reward and a future incentive. You'll live up to his confidence in your performance to come.

Above all, keep it friendly, positive, and smile. I know it's hard, but he is probably more apt to grant you what you wish out of benevolence rather than being bullied.

If this doesn't work, he'll think he still has your good will as you quietly test the market for better positions.

. . . .

Best Practice 68
Selling Services?
Offer a Plain-Wrap Version

The other day I was approached by someone who wants a webinar speaker, and I am an experienced one, in addition to being a conventional platform type. But he wanted to pay less than my prevailing rate for a performance.

I mentioned that the 75–90-minute event that he had in mind would require far more than 75–90 minutes for me to craft and to deliver.

Not only is there setup time on the day of the event to make sure the computer equipment, sound levels, and screens are working correctly, but I will need decompression time after being on stage (albeit an electronic one) for that sustained period.

Plus, that day cannot be sold to anyone else who is willing to pay full price for it.

Anyway, he wasn't biting.

Then I told him about my background and how by being a best-selling author in the subject area, I had already created awareness among millions of people of my credibility. I also had unique ideas, and he could promote these strengths and attractive qualities.

He seemed indifferent to my marquis value, pretending he was only interested in a generic talking head who could deliver 75–90 minutes of baffling banter.

So I made him this offer: I would consider doing the program for close to his budget providing he (1) sold my audios and videos so I could recoup my investment, or (2) agreed to not use my name or any reference to me in promoting his event.

In other words, if he wants a discounted plain-wrap speaker, somewhat like a store brand of ketchup or mayonnaise, then he can bargain for that. Just don't tell your clients they're getting Kraft or Best Foods or Heinz.

From a negotiation standpoint, this separates the wheat from the chaff. If they really want *you*, they should pay your prevailing rate, because they'll be getting the full benefit, including your marquis value, reputation, credibility, and drawing power.

But if they truly don't care, you can give them something less pricey, but they can't advertise you as the national or international brand that you are.

There are famous actors who appear in small independent films, in noncredited roles. They're in the pictures, to be sure, but their names don't appear in the credits. This is because they have donated their time or worked for far less than their customary contract value, so producers cannot tout their presence as they sell their films to distributors and the public.

Try this gambit of plain-wrapping yourself when you're negotiating, and see which version they buy.

· · · · · · · · · · · · · ·

Best Practice 69
Avoid Doing Business with Troubled Businesses

It's simply good business to do business with companies that are going to be around for a while, that don't have both feet firmly planted on banana peels.

Besides seeking out their credit ratings, are there any tip-offs that they're in trouble?

Typically, they try to enforce every agreement to the letter and extract every dime they can from you.

For instance, recently a travel company didn't want to give me a refund when I had to reschedule a trip. I had already spent a good amount of money with this online entity, but it insisted on dinging me a huge amount for changing my plans. Obviously they didn't care that I travel quite a lot and the future value of my patronage far outstripped the amount they were penalizing me.

Their future was flaky, so they didn't mind burning their clients.

Another instance: I needed to bolt out of a restaurant that I had frequented for more than a dozen years. I flagged the server and asked if I could cancel the entrée and simply pay for my salad and drink. She disappeared.

A full twenty minutes later, she reappeared with plate in hand. She said it was too late to cancel: "You can always take it home with you."

Clearly it didn't take twenty minutes to cook a steak. There was plenty of time to cancel it, but that would have reduced the size of the check and her tip. She simply didn't want to accommodate me and felt she had a right to force me to consume the meal as originally ordered.

The price of the entrée was only $39.

I spent thousands elsewhere avoiding that place.

I recall terminating an Internet-access subscription that came bundled with my PC. I was transferred to a guy who harshly interrogated me and tried to impose an unjustified cancellation fee. I vowed never to come back, and I explicitly said it was no way to do business.

That same company is no longer in the Internet access business. No wonder.

Often, when companies drive hard bargains with their clients, or they insist on collecting large penalties or strictly interpreting the fine print in their user agreements, they're in financial trouble. If you believe they're acting in a shortsighted way, they are, because they can no longer see a long-term relationship. They sense they won't be around, so they're not going to leave a thing on the table.

That's a good cue to pick up your chips and walk away.

. . . .

Best Practice 70
Ask, "What Can We Agree On?"

Offended by a prospective purchaser of her home in an upscale town in Southern California, the seller rejected his offer outright, communicating through her broker that she didn't want to see another offer from that "so-and-so."

Too bad, because the property is truly something unique and special, with attributes you just don't see everyday or everywhere. What killed the deal?

The buyer wanted to get a concession, which constituted a mere fraction of the overall cost of obtaining the property.

It reminds one of the old proverb about the horseshoe nail: For want of a nail, the shoe was lost; for want of the shoe, the horse was lost; for want of the horse, the rider was lost; for want of the rider, the battle was lost; for want of the battle, the kingdom was lost. All for want of a horseshoe nail.

Piddling things account for so many undone deals, so many dashed hopes, and so many ruffled feathers and bruised egos.

How can we avoid such unpleasantness and seal more deals?

Try this line before you break off your negotiations: "What can we *agree* on?"

This serves three purposes:

1. It focuses the parties on consensus, reminding them of what is *not* in question.

2. It shows minor concerns to be just that—minor.
3. It enables both parties to sound positive, which is hard to do in a defensive atmosphere.

So before storming away or feeling insulted, try just once to find areas of agreement.

It could be all you need to get back on track!

. . . .

Best Practice 71
Ask for the Moon and You Might Get It

As a PhD candidate, I unearthed a skinny book of behavioral research findings that contained some true gems of wisdom.

One of my favorites pertains to persuasion. It applies both to selling and to negotiating, and by putting it to use I have done very well, thank you.

Simply put, this nugget says: "If you ask for more, you'll get more; and if you ask for less, you'll get less."

Doesn't this fly in the face of those who promote modesty, who maintain that if you ask for little, just a pittance, you'll be less likely to be rejected? Aren't the meek supposed to inherit the earth?

Yes, this notion does disagree with those who would take a humbler path. Just as that senior character in the play and movie *The Producers*, proclaimed, "If you've got it; flaunt it!" this adage could say, "If you're good, ask for twice or three times what you'll accept!"

I recall doing this when I was negotiating a videotape deal with a major studio. I asked for triple what I would have accepted for the one-day shooting, simply as a fun and provocative negotiating gambit.

You can imagine how stunned I was when my counterpart thought for about fifteen seconds and replied, "I believe we can do that!"

Try this for yourself.

If they really want you or the value you're offering, they won't flatly reject your request, and some will even take you up on it.

. . . .

Best Practice 72
Define the Situation Your Way

I returned to the parking lot at my client's site to see that my rented car had a huge dent in the driver's door. Immediately, from that rooftop location, I phoned my insurance agent to check my coverage. He said that I had a $1,000 deductible under my collision coverage, so it was likely that I'd be out of pocket for the entire repair.

I probed. Why was this a collision issue? He told me that collision covers one-party accidents, like driving your car into a tree.

"But I didn't cause the dent!" I countered. Then an insight hit me.

"Jim, what is 'comprehensive,' then?"

"That's when a tree falls down in a storm and hits your car."

"Does comprehensive cover vandalism?"

"Yes, it does."

"Jim, I can't tell you exactly how that dent got there, but it's possible someone didn't like the way I parked and kicked the door, making that half-moon crater. If that happened, how much is my comprehensive deductible?"

"Let's check . . . That's only $250."

"Well, Jim, let's call this *comprehensive*, OK?"

We did, and my credit card picked up the first $250 of liability as part of my platinum membership, so the incident didn't cost me a dime.

Characterization is the art and practice of defining something in terms more favorable to yourself, your company, or your cause. Lawyers learn this art in school and on the job. Everyone should.

By the way, what's the difference between "tax avoidance" and "tax evasion?"

About five to fifteen years in prison!

Seriously: every American citizen is entitled to lawfully avoid and minimize his tax burdens. The great jurist Learned Hand said it is a citizen's *duty*. But no one has the right to illegally *evade* paying their taxes.

What's the practical difference?

Often, whether an item is deductible boils down to a matter of characterization.

Learn to characterize creatively, and your negotiations will be much more rewarding.

. . . .

Best Practice 73
Learn Contract Law

The client ordered a series of six speeches from me at a total fee of $48,000, plus expenses.

I did the first one successfully. The evaluations were splendid, and I was looking forward to doing the rest in the sequence, about one per week for the next five weeks.

Suddenly everything was thrown into a cocked hat. My contact informed me by phone that his company wanted to pay me for the one I had done, but cancel the following five.

At first, I was flummoxed. My presentation was a success, but they wished to terminate the deal? It didn't add up.

After probing for the reason, it was disclosed to me that I had an enemy in the firm, someone from long ago with whom I had a dispute. And he threatened the parent company with I-don't-know-what if they didn't sever ties with me.

Once I heard the story, I decided to enforce our contract.

"If you don't want to proceed with all six speeches," I said, "You can pay me for them, plus my out-of-pocket expenses to date. If not, I'll consider it a breach of contract, and I'll be forced to take legal action."

Within two weeks, I received the full amount I was due under the terms of our agreement.

That contract may seem not so large today, but let me put it into perspective for you. My entire law-school tuition cost me—guess what?

That's right: $48,000!

So because I knew and was able to enforce my contractual rights, *that one deal paid me back for attending law school.*

Now I'm not saying *you* should go. It is a huge commitment, and while I was able to maintain a six-figure consulting practice while I attended, for most students, it's simply not possible to succeed in law school and to earn big bucks at the same time.

But there is no excuse for not taking a college-level course in business law. They're available everywhere, in university extension programs as well as in the regular curriculum.

Among other topics, you'll learn some essentials about how contracts are formed, modified, executed, broken, and remedied when breaches in performance occur. All of which will make you a savvier negotiator and will enable you to take on more reasonable risks.

From my training and experience with contract law, I am often able to compose much more informal, yet still sufficiently binding, agreements than the folks I encounter. I can use what seems to be everyday language to weave together deals, words, and phrases that enable my counterparts to relax and feel less threatened than they do when forced to sign off on texts that read like legalese. We reach faster agreements, get the wheels of progress turning, and talk through any issues that may come up later.

Without at least some legal training, you don't know what you're missing, and that can be a very costly void.

. . . .

Best Practice 74
Ask, "Where Did We Go Wrong?"

When negotiations break down, both parties can lose. But sometimes you can pick up the pieces.

I responded to a consulting inquiry from a top New York modeling agency that wanted to improve its marketing capabilities. After submitting a proposal, I heard nothing—zilch—and I couldn't seem to get my contact on the phone.

So I did something novel: I drafted a "Where did we go wrong?" letter. Those five words appeared in the first line in 16-point type. I went on to calmly state that I am in the business of building sales and customer service, so I try to be especially alert to our own shortcomings. "Please," I went on to ask, "tell us where we missed the mark in failing to serve your needs."

Within a week I received a phone call from a different person in the organization, who was very polite and pleasant. Instead of reciting my many faults, she simply picked up the pieces and retained my services. We ended up doing a very successful nationwide campaign that was very interesting and lucrative. All because I got the idea of not accepting failure as being final.

Try this technique a few weeks or a month after negotiations break down.

Providing there is still a flicker of interest, you might be able to quickly move things back to the front burner.

. . . .

Best Practice 75
Find a Way to Say Yes

I have been going back and forth, exchanging emails with a potential seminar sponsor a world away. Although it's very possible that we may never do business, I won't give in to that initial perception.

If I've learned anything in a few decades of professional speaking, management consulting, and publishing, it's this: "There is a way to make every deal."

Don't get me wrong. If someone approaches me to do a program 12,000 miles away and expects me to charge only for the single hour or day that the speech consumes, then I'll have to decline. But I won't really say no.

I might say, "I'd love to do this program and help you out, but I'm going to need more billable time once I arrive, to justify the four days that will be consumed in traveling to and from. So if you can keep me busy with paid engagements for a number of days, let's see what we can put together!"

An outright declination leaves them only with a problem: where are they going to find a capable presenter?

But my response offers a solution. It entices my counterpart to think, "How could we do that?" In other words, it generates a win-win situation instead of lose-lose.

This has worked for me, and it has made my hosts very happy. So try it out!

. . . .

Best Practice 76
Don't Get Defensive

Defensiveness is responding to nearly everything we hear as if it is a personal attack. It's like the flu: one party gets it, and it spreads.

There are six messages negotiators use, accidentally or purposely, that cause defensive reactions:

1. Evaluation
2. Control
3. Strategy
4. Neutrality
5. Superiority
6. Certainty

Look at these actual statements people have made in negotiations. See if you can peg which of the six defensive messages applies.

We simply can't do that!

Looks a lot like certainty, doesn't it? The tip-off is the "can't" word. It sounds conclusive, doesn't it?

I must get $800,000 for this property!

Certainty again!

I don't like your negotiating style!

That is a personal attack. Notice how it refers to the other person, to "your style." This sounds like evaluation to me.

Defensive messages get negotiators offtrack and onto defending their threatened egos.

Instead of using defensive phrases, we should be using supportive alternatives. There are six of these. When we stick to them, we tend to reduce conflicts and personality clashes:

1. Description
2. Problem and solution focus
3. Spontaneity
4. Empathy
5. Equality
6. Flexibility

Here is an astonishingly supportive phrase:

Gee, I'm sorry to hear you say that. Let's see where we can go from here.

Gee is spontaneous.

I'm sorry is empathic.

To hear you say that acknowledges that you heard what was uttered. You're using nonjudgmental description.

Let's implies equality, inviting both parties to join together.

See where we can go from here suggests a problem and solution focus, and it also sounds flexible.

Using supportive words and phrases will do two essential things for you. It will prevent defensiveness, and if defensiveness has already been aroused, it will reduce it.

· · · · · · · · · · · · · ·

Best Practice 77
Remember: Picasso and Google Didn't Become Rich Working by the Hour

I write some of my best articles, books, and coaching and consulting proposals in the wee hours of the morning, long before dawn.

Officially, this is not during a 9-5 business day, is it?

What if I wanted to sell these precious hours to an employer on the grounds that this is when I perform best? Do you think I could line up a job, say with a publisher, to come into headquarters between 1 and 5 in the morning?

Probably not, right? After all, who is going to supervise me? Will the lights and air conditioning even function at that time?

No, most employers implicitly say to creative people: create when we want you to, when we're here, or else. Isn't this just a little unrealistic, if not counterproductive? But it's just one way in which the working world structures work based on artificial criteria.

Let's delve even deeper into the mysteries of the way work is defined, offered, and managed.

For instance, I don't know anybody who is paid by the idea, yet ideas are supremely important, right?

There is this legendary story about Coca-Cola, invented by a pharmacist in a small town. One day someone came to him and asked, "Have you ever thought of bottling it?"

That simple, elegant idea had never occurred to the druggist. But you know what happened to Coke after it was bottled, right?

How do you monetize and get paid a proper fee for an idea? This is an open question, and it begs for a negotiated answer. Most of us are not, will not be, and cannot be paid by the idea, though ideas are the ushers of innovation and profits.

Similarly, good judgment is crucial to the success of an enterprise, but do you know people who are paid by the opinion, except judges in the legal system and those folks on TV that judge talent?

I was called by a former client, who asked me whether I thought a certain electronic device could be profitably sold over the phone. I replied that I needed to meet with him for a day to become familiar with the device, the pricing, and so forth.

"Nah," he replied, "you're a pro; just give me your gut reaction!"

My gut said, "Don't do it; this can't be sold over the phone at a profit."

But I bit my tongue, and he went off and lost millions trying to sell it that way.

Was my expert opinion worth a fractional amount of his losses? Today his reply would have to be a resounding yes. But businesspeople aren't used to paying by the opinion, by the judgment—or, as in this example, by the warning. Typically, ideas and judgments are devalued because we simply aren't comfortable conceiving of professional services in ways that aren't delineated by clock time.

I saw a film about the famous artist Pablo Picasso. He worked so fast it was amazing—finishing drawings and paintings in mere minutes. Should he have charged by the minute or by the hour for his art? Could he have paid the rent that way?

Google grew to become one of the most profitable enterprises in the world, doing something no company had even conceived before 1993, when the Internet became operational: charging by the click.

Here's the Best Practices learning point: *we need to devise novel ways to charge and to be paid for our contributions, and to justify our pricing by recognition of the value they bestow*, not based on the time or place in which the work was performed.

If you can do this, you are on your way to success, and very possibly to riches.

One of my clients is himself a consultant. He helps his employers to save money on their Yellow Page advertising. Typically he'll reduce the size of their ads but increase their effectiveness. He doesn't charge by the hour or by the day.

They save money on their ads and pay him a percentage of their first year's advertising savings. That's a creative way to work together.

Use your imagination to devise similar win-win reward systems.

. . . .

Bonus Best Practice
Practice, Practice, Practice!

This may be self-serving, because I am a producer of courses on negotiation, but I believe everyone—all adults, consumers, and businesspeople—should seek formal negotiation training.

I say this for at least five reasons:

1. It levels the playing field when it comes to skills and knowledge.
2. It becomes very difficult for one party to exploit a ploy without being detected and corrected.
3. It slows the arms race by taking the "nukes" of impulsiveness and impatience out of the equation.
4. It enables participants to focus on deal points instead of steal points.
5. It teaches people that there are many ways to agree if the participants are civil.

When it becomes clear to both sides in a negotiation that they are equally savvy, many of the gimmicks, ploys, and dirty tricks are implicitly discouraged. This is helpful all around, because it reinforces the serious purpose that is to be served through good-faith bargaining.

I've written a book entitled *The Law of Large Numbers: How to Make Success Inevitable.*

It operates from a simple concept: do something many times—nearly any human activity—and you'll get better at it. Significantly surpass that amount of endeavor, and you'll probably become expert. Keep going, adding repetitions, and you may become rich. Ultimately, if you do more than anyone else, you'll become a legend.

Above I mentioned Picasso, one of my favorite artists. I'll name a few more: Erté, Chagall, Dali, and Miró. What do they have in common? They were incredibly prolific, minting various artifacts, often in multiple media. As they aged, they kept producing, some into their nineties.

If you doubt what I'm saying about how the Law of Large Numbers creates success, look up a book by Dr. Srully Blotnick: *Growing Rich Your Own Way.* He studied rich people and found they had made it in nearly every walk of life. Riches came to them once they performed the mechanics of their occupations repeatedly and stayed in their fields over time. It didn't require genius or special savvy, but a genuine interest in and a long-term commitment to their worth. Often, wealth sneaked up on them. They were unaware of how their wealth was growing.

Negotiation operates in much the same manner. Do a lot of it, and you'll improve, especially when using the theories and practices I have offered in this book.

Earlier, I wrote about how car dealers get the jump on buyers. They negotiate *every day*, often multiple times within a day, setting prices, purchasing used cars, dickering over financing options, and appraising body damage.

How can they *not* beat that pants off of people who walk into a dealership once or twice over the course of many years?

There's an old joke about the fellow on the sidewalks of New York who asked another chap, "How do you get to Carnegie Hall?"

"Practice!" he heard back.

Today I went to see a new movie, which was quite beautiful, filmed mostly in Venice. The experience was partially marred by a glaring imperfection in the center of the screen, a tear of some kind. Mind you, this is a modern theater, advertising the most advanced digital sound quality, yet the screen was blemished enough to require me to make an effort to block it out.

I was with my wife, and we were on a "date," so I didn't want to ruin our moods by haggling with theater management before we left.

But as I see it, they owed us something, having delivered less than a completely enjoyable experience.

This was an opportunity to negotiate, perhaps for two free passes to a future showing. Moreover, it was a chance to inform management that their theater is falling below standards, and people are noticing.

Having had this happen just two hours ago, I may still call them. Even if I get no satisfaction, I will garner some practice in negotiating.

Another way to practice is to constantly negotiate and renegotiate your aspirations. Every day we set out to accomplish certain tasks, to pursue various goals. Are they high enough? Do they challenge you sufficiently?

Calibrate your dreams to levels that are slightly, or even significantly, beyond your reach.

In other words, *go for more, for continuous improvement.*

Let me give you an example. As a consultant, I am always hunting for the next client. Unfortunately, this objective is thwarted by my existing clients, inasmuch as it's hard to find new deals when I am focusing on executing the ones that are already on the books.

But there is a way current clients can make my marketing more successful. It is by writing me a letter of recommendation for general distribution, once they are seeing that my tips, techniques, and programs are succeeding. The ideal time to request a letter or a reference is not after you have earned it, in the traditional sense.

The best moment is during your primary negotiations, before you have undertaken any work. Here's what I say:

"I rely on my satisfied clients to stand up for me and recommend me to future prospects, so when we are reaching a level of success and you are convinced I am imparting value, would you kindly write me a brief paragraph or two attesting to that, something I can show to my future clients?"

I've never had someone decline. However, when I have asked later on without this agreement in place, many have hesitated to disclose the success we have reached.

Perhaps in the absence of any other motivation, they felt paying me my contract price was sufficient.

That's understandable, and it's my fault. I should have inserted this as a requirement of the original deal. By asking for more, especially early on, you'll get more.

But you won't ask for more until and unless you raise your aspiration levels. First, you have to believe you are worth something more. So practice negotiating with yourself!

Let me say few things about failure. It too is inevitable if you work the Law of Large Numbers, and engage in more negotiations than you do at present. That's life, so learn to accept the bad with the good.

One of my clients, a Fortune 500 company, sold a pricey package of computer hardware and software. They used to tell a grim joke around headquarters: "There are five steps that are taken in getting a client on the books. The sixth step is the inevitable lawsuit that follows."

Of course they were overstating the problem, but legal hassles were frequent enough that the gallows humor wasn't totally inappropriate.

The point is that the company was prepared for that eventuality. They turned enough deals and grew so fast that there was bound to be some collateral damage. They negotiated with themselves in advance about what to expect and what failures they would have to cope with. As a result, they were prepared instead of daunted when setbacks occurred.

Follow their lead. Prepare for everything by outpracticing everyone else!

Epilogue

When I've Blown It—
A Negotiator's Retrospective

I told you I'd admit to my failures.

I think there are a few purposes to be served by it. For one thing, you need to know that nobody is a perfect negotiator. Every author and pundit you find has an unpublished list of losing transactions, or at least deals that he wishes he could have modified, avoided, or seized instead of letting go.

The second purpose is to encourage you to always maintain a certain amount of modesty, no matter how much arrogance your income at a given time might seem to justify.

One of my all-time favorite examples of a blown negotiation comes from a failed video contract with a major media company, a division of a large TV network. I was approached by a senior executive who asked me if I was interested in taping a half hour program in one of my areas of expertise. When asked how much of an advance against royalties I wanted, I pulled a very high number out of nowhere and calmly delivered it to her.

She paused for a second and then replied: "I think we can do that."

She mailed me a contract that I put into the hands of my highly paid attorney. He found something he didn't like—a clause that seemed to make me liable for any accidents that occurred on the set during taping.

We contested that point with the studio. Some acrimony resulted, and the deal was suddenly off.

At the time I didn't know, and my attorney should have realized, that I could have purchased a low-cost indemnity insurance policy to cover the unlikely occurrences from which the studio was trying to protect itself. (See Best Practice 44: Get a Third Party to Pay.)

Given the amount of advance I was receiving, the prestige of the studio connection, and the potential sales that would accrue, it was a tiny amount of dough to invest. To this day, I regret how this transaction turned out, and no amount of rationalizing can make me feel better about it.

I blew it in three ways: by investing my attorney with the credibility to effectively nix the deal based on a minor clause; by misjudging the value of the overall deal and the relative insignificance of the contractual point in question; and by having "my lawyer talk with your lawyer." I took the power to make a deal out of the hands of the people who really wanted to make one and put it into the hands of those who make it a point to break deals.

(I started law school soon thereafter, partly motivated by this mishap.)

On another occasion, a former client of mine asked me to do a consulting project, and I submitted a proposal with a price tag of about $300,000.

He came back to me and said, "My budget is only $100,000," and he wouldn't budge from that position. He wanted what I had proposed for about a third of the price.

So far you might be thinking he was being unreasonable. At the time, that was precisely my view. Plus, I was peeved that he would grind me on price, knowing how capable I was of doing projects of the sort that he needed.

Anyway, refer back to Best Practice 51: "Play the Shell Game and Win." That is precisely what I should have done to make the offered $100,000 agreeable.

As it turned out, about two years later I heard from this fellow, who was beating the bushes, seeking employment. He had awarded the contract to another consulting company that fell on its face and failed to deliver as I would have done. I sensed that this gent would have still been employed if I had been selected in that competitor's place.

This is a typical lose-lose outcome, something that occurs much of the time in negotiations. Each party takes a hard position, refusing to concede or find a creative alternative, and neither gets anything good as a result.

Twice I blew large consulting contracts because I was in a hurry to catch a plane or to beat traffic. The prospects blurted out something they needed to have—in one circumstance, a noncompete agreement.

I replied, nearly out of breath, "OK, I'll need one, too!"

We never got to that point.

Did I actually need a reciprocal noncompete agreement? Probably not, but the person who pulled out this requirement was also a lawyer, and I suppose my professional ego flared and made me strut my stuff and play verbal tag with him. Best Practice 33: Don't Be Impulsive might have helped me there.

Is there a central theme to my shortfalls as a negotiator? Looking back, I see at least one that I can encapsulate this way:

I regret the deals I declined to make much more than the deals I did make, no matter how deficient the latter initially seemed to be.

Simply put, I'd like to have that money I passed up sitting in a mutual fund. By now its value would be denominated in the millions.

More deals are better than fewer, because they lead to yet more opportunities.

For instance, I can trace more than $1 million of consulting fees I earned to a book buyer in Tacoma, Washington. He liked one of my books so much that he passed it to his sales manager, who read it and phoned my office. That contact led to an $80,000 contract with the company they worked for.

One day, when I was delivering a seminar, the president observed for about ten minutes. A few years later, he was tapped to become CEO of yet a larger firm, and he brought me in to do about $500,000 worth of work. That engagement led to a few other deals based on the tools I had devised for him and his new outfit.

Big oak trees come from little acorns, says an old adage. And it's true.

We disparage little deals at our peril, not only because they put bread on the table, but because they lead to even bigger opportunities.

If you are a baseball fan, you might have come across the book *Moneyball*, also a motion picture starring Brad Pitt. Billy Beane, the general manager of the Oakland Athletics, is featured, and he is renowned for his negotiation savvy.

Speaking about one of his peers when he was playing ball, Lenny Dykstra, Beane said he was an ideal athlete. Among other attributes, he had the uncanny ability to put his failures, especially his strikeouts as a batter, behind him. For Dykstra, when a game was done, it was really over.

Beane admits it was the opposite for him. He ruminates over his past miscues, taking his head out of today's game, leading to slumps.

I don't want to do that here by recounting the times I blew it, so I'll stop here, with the instances I have provided. To that end, as negotiators, I hope you and I become more like Dykstra and less like Beane. But we should be aware that there are no perfect negotiators or ballplayers, and the best hitters fail seven times out of ten. If they just do that consistently, over the course of a fifteen- or twenty-year career, they make it to the Hall of Fame.

Keep plugging away, as I urge you to do in the Bonus Best Practice.

Before long, you'll find yourself at the top!

Afterword

Thank you for reading this book! I hope you find these practices not only useful but confidence building and enjoyable. Feel free to contact me about any additional help I can give you and your organization in the form of consulting, coaching, and keynote speaking.

We're not only consultants in negotiation but in selling and customer satisfaction.

In the meantime, good luck!

Best,
GARY
Dr. Gary S. Goodman

www.drgarygoodman.com
gary@drgarygoodman.com
www.customersatisfaction.com
gary@customersatisfaction.com

www.negotiationschool.com
gary@negotiationschool.com
www.drgarygoodman.com
gary@drgarygoodman.com
(818) 970-GARY (4279)

Printed in the USA
CPSIA information can be obtained
at www.ICGtesting.com
JSHW012029140824
68134JS00033B/2961